Table of Contents

1 Chapter 1: The Weight of Stone

The coolness of the granite under my fingertips, a subtle shift in texture, a hidden flaw—these are the whispers of stone. They are the first words in a conversation that unfolds between myself and the material. Before any tool touches the surface, there's this initial intimacy, a sensing of the stone's inherent nature. I run my hands across its rough exterior, tracing the contours of its form, feeling the weight of its history. This is not simply a block of granite; it is a vessel of compressed time, a fragment of the earth's ancient story waiting to be revealed. This initial encounter, this tactile exploration, sets the stage for everything that follows. It's a process of understanding, not just the physical properties of the stone, but also its potential, its hidden spirit.

The density of basalt, the crystalline structure of quartz, the subtle veining in marble – each variety of stone possesses a unique character. This individuality demands a specific approach, a tailored dialogue. Working with alabaster, for instance, requires a delicate touch, a sensitivity to its translucence and fragility. It's a dance of subtle pressures, a gentle coaxing of form from the material. Conversely, tackling a block of granite demands strength, persistence, and a willingness to engage in a more forceful exchange. The tools become extensions of the body, transmitting the energy needed to shape this unyielding substance. The resistance offered by the stone isn't an obstacle; it's a vital part of the creative process, a challenge that informs and refines the final form.

This exchange, this back-and-forth between sculptor and stone, is where the true magic happens. It's not a matter of imposing a preconceived idea onto the material, but rather a collaborative effort. I listen to the stone, responding to its inherent qualities, allowing its natural form to guide my hand. Sometimes, a hidden fissure reveals a new possibility, suggesting a curve or an angle I hadn't initially envisioned. Other times, the sheer weight of the stone dictates the direction of the work, grounding the piece in a sense of gravity and permanence. This responsiveness to the material, this willingness to adapt and evolve, is crucial to creating a sculpture that feels authentic and alive.

The act of sculpting is, in essence, a process of revelation. It's not about creating something from nothing, but rather uncovering the form that already exists within the stone. I chip away at the excess, gradually revealing the hidden figure, the nascent landscape, the waiting form. Each strike of the chisel, each pass of the rasp, brings me closer to the essence of the piece. It's a subtractive process, a paring down to the essential, a stripping away of the superfluous. The final form isn't something I've imposed; it's something I've discovered, something that was always there, waiting to be brought to light.

And within this process of discovery, there's a profound sense of connection. I become intimately familiar with the stone, its textures, its imperfections, its strengths. My hands learn its language, understanding the nuances of its response to each tool, each gesture. This intimate knowledge, this deep understanding of the material, allows me to push the boundaries of what's possible, to coax forth forms that surprise and delight. The stone ceases to be an inanimate object and becomes a partner in creation, a collaborator in a shared journey of exploration.

This dialogue with matter extends beyond the purely physical. As I work, my thoughts, emotions, and memories become embedded in the stone. The frustration of a difficult cut, the joy of a breakthrough, the quiet contemplation of a subtle curve – all these experiences leave their mark. The sculpture becomes a repository of these moments, a tangible record of the creative process. It's not just a representation of an idea, but an embodiment of the journey itself.

This intimate connection with the material is what gives stone sculpture its unique power. It's the weight of the stone, its resistance to change, its enduring presence, that anchors the work in a sense of timelessness. The sculpture becomes a testament to the enduring nature of both the material and the human spirit, a tangible expression of the dialogue between artist and earth. And in this dialogue, in this intimate exchange, we find not only the weight of stone, but also its profound and enduring beauty. The stone holds within it the echoes of ancient forces, the whispers of geological time. And as we shape it, we become part of that story, adding our own voice to the ongoing narrative of creation. This is the essence of sculpting, the heart of the conversation between stone and spirit. It's a conversation that transcends words, spoken in the language of form, texture, and the enduring presence of the material itself. This conversation continues long after the sculptor's hand has rested, resonating in the silent presence of the finished work.

1.1 Form and Feeling

The sculptor's hand, guided by intuition and honed by practice, seeks not merely to impose form upon stone, but to uncover the form already residing within. It's a dance of discovery, a conversation between artist and material. We tap into the stone's inherent qualities, its density, its texture, its color, allowing these elements to inform our creative decisions. A vein of quartz might suggest a flowing line, a cluster of crystals a point of emphasis. This responsiveness to the material is crucial. It transforms the act of sculpting from a mechanical process into an intimate exchange, a merging of intention and inherent form.

This inherent form, however, is not a fixed entity. It is a potential waiting to be realized, a whisper that requires amplification. We bring our own experiences, emotions, and perceptions to the stone, projecting our inner world onto its silent surface. A sense of joy might be expressed through a sweeping curve, a feeling of grief through a rough, unfinished texture. The stone, in turn, reflects these emotions back to us, amplifying and transforming them in unexpected ways. The resulting sculpture becomes a tangible record of this intimate dialogue, a fusion of the material and the immaterial.

Consider the weight of a hand resting on a block of marble. The coolness of the stone, its unyielding mass, these are tactile sensations that inform our understanding of the material. But beyond the purely physical, there is an emotional resonance, a sense of connection to something ancient and enduring. This connection deepens as we begin to work the stone, chipping away at its surface, revealing the hidden forms within. We find ourselves drawn into a meditative state, a state of heightened awareness where the distinction between self and material begins to blur.

The act of sculpting is not solely about imposing our will upon the stone. It is also about surrendering to its inherent properties, allowing the material to guide our hand and inform our decisions. This requires a certain degree of humility, a willingness to let go of preconceived notions and embrace the unexpected. We must be open to the possibility that the stone has something to teach us, that it possesses a wisdom that transcends our own limited understanding. In this sense, sculpting becomes a collaborative process, a conversation between equals.

This dialogue extends beyond the purely physical realm. As we work the stone, we engage in a process of self-discovery, exploring the hidden depths of our own emotions and experiences. The sculpture becomes a mirror, reflecting back to us the nuances of our inner world. We see ourselves in the curves and contours of the stone, in the rough textures and polished surfaces. The act of creation becomes an act of self-reflection, a journey into the heart of our own being.
The finished sculpture, then, is not simply an object, but a vessel of meaning, a tangible embodiment of the dialogue between artist and material. It speaks to us of the intimate connection between form and feeling, of the transformative power of creative expression. It reminds us that beauty can be found in the most unexpected places, that even the hardest of materials can be imbued with emotion and meaning. It is a testament to the enduring power of human creativity, our capacity to shape not only the world around us, but also the world within. And in this shaping, we find not just form, but a deeper understanding of ourselves and our place in the universe. This understanding, this connection, is the essence of sculpting, the heart of the dialogue between stone and spirit. The process unfolds, a slow unveiling of the inner life of the stone, a gentle coaxing of form from the formless, and a profound reflection of the sculptor's own journey.

1.2 The Stone's Voice

Every stone possesses a unique resonance, a subtle vibration that speaks to the attentive sculptor. This isn't a mystical claim, but a recognition of the deep interplay between the material world and our own sensibilities. Consider the cool, smooth surface of marble, how it yields to the chisel yet retains an inherent strength. Contrast this with the rough, porous texture of sandstone, its warmth radiating even in the coldest studio. These qualities aren't simply physical attributes; they are expressive potentials, whispers of the stone's own history and character. Understanding this voice, learning to listen to the subtle language of stone, is fundamental to the sculptor's craft. It's a conversation that begins with touch, with the feeling of the material against the skin, the resistance it offers to the tools. It's in this intimate exchange that the true dialogue with matter begins.

This dialogue is a reciprocal process. We impose our will upon the stone, shaping it according to our vision. Yet the stone, in turn, shapes us. Its inherent limitations, its unique characteristics, guide our hands and influence our decisions. A flaw in the marble might redirect the flow of a curve, a particularly hard patch of granite might necessitate a change in approach. These are not impediments, but opportunities. They are the stone's contributions to the conversation, its way of pushing back, of asserting its own presence in the creative process. Through this interplay of intention and resistance, a new form emerges, a synthesis of the sculptor's vision and the stone's inherent nature. This is the essence of the stone's voice:

a subtle, persistent influence that shapes both the artwork and the artist.

The sculptor's ability to discern this voice hinges on an intimate familiarity with their material. This goes beyond simply knowing the hardness or density of a particular stone. It involves understanding its geological origins, the forces that shaped it over millennia, the subtle variations in color and texture that tell a story of its journey through time. For example, a vein of quartz running through granite speaks of intense heat and pressure deep within the earth. A fossil embedded in limestone reveals a glimpse of ancient life. These are not mere details, but narratives etched into the very fabric of the stone. They enrich the sculptor's understanding, adding layers of meaning to the dialogue. By recognizing these narratives, the sculptor can incorporate them into their work, allowing the stone's history to inform the final form.

This deep understanding comes not from textbooks or lectures, but from direct experience, from countless hours spent observing, touching, and working with the material. It's a process of immersion, of becoming attuned to the subtle nuances of the stone's character. It's about developing a sensitivity to the way light plays across its surface, the way it feels under the chisel, the sound it makes when struck. This sensory engagement is essential to truly hearing the stone's voice. It's through this intimate connection that we can move beyond the purely technical aspects of sculpting and enter into a creative partnership with the material itself.

Ultimately, the stone's voice is not a literal sound, but a metaphor for the deep connection between the sculptor and their material. It's a recognition of the stone's agency in the creative process, its ability to shape not only the final form of the sculpture, but also the artist's understanding of the world. This dialogue is an ongoing exploration, a constant interplay between intention and discovery. It's a journey that leads not only to the creation of beautiful objects, but also to a deeper appreciation of the profound interconnectedness of all things. The stone whispers secrets of the earth, of time, and of the very forces that shape our existence. It is up to the sculptor to listen, to interpret, and to translate those whispers into a language that can be shared with the world. This act of translation, this giving voice to the silent eloquence of stone, is at the heart of the sculptor's art. It's a process of revealing the hidden narratives embedded within the material, bringing forth the stories that lie dormant within the earth. By embracing this dialogue, the sculptor not only creates art, but also participates in a continuous conversation with the world around them, a conversation that enriches both the artist and the observer.

1.3 A Dialogue with Matter

The sculptor's dialogue with matter isn't a monologue of imposition, but a conversation, a give-and-take. We don't simply force stone to our will; we listen to its suggestions. We learn its language of fracture and flow, its whispers of density and translucence. Each type of stone possesses a unique personality, a distinct vocabulary. Granite, with its formidable strength, demands respect, its crystalline structure dictating the rhythm of the chisel. Alabaster, by contrast, invites a gentler touch, its softness allowing for intricate detail, a luminous whisper of form emerging from within. This inherent character of the material isn't a limitation, but an inspiration, a starting point for the creative journey. It's in understanding these inherent properties that we begin to truly collaborate with the stone.

Consider the process of selecting a block. We walk among the raw materials, hands grazing surfaces, feeling for the energy within. This tactile exploration is crucial. We are not simply choosing a size or shape; we are seeking a partner in creation. The weight, the texture, the subtle variations in color and veining, all speak to us, hinting at the forms they hold within. A particular curve might suggest a shoulder, a fissure a flowing drape. The stone itself begins to participate in the creative process, offering suggestions, whispering possibilities. This initial encounter is the first exchange in a long and intimate conversation.

Once chosen, the stone is brought to the studio, where the dialogue continues. We begin by removing excess material, a process of subtraction that reveals the form within. Each strike of the chisel, each pass of the rasp, is a response to the stone's resistance and surrender. We are not merely imposing a pre-conceived image; we are discovering it, uncovering it, in collaboration with the material. The stone guides our hand, revealing its inherent structure, its natural inclinations. This process is a dance, a delicate interplay between intention and responsiveness.

The sculptor's tools become extensions of our senses, amplifying our ability to perceive and respond to the nuances of the material. The point chisel allows us to define sharp lines, to carve crisp edges. The toothed chisel, with its rhythmic bite, creates texture and depth. The rasp, with its abrasive surface, refines and smooths. Each tool offers a different way of interacting with the stone, a different mode of communication. They are the instruments through which we translate our vision into tangible form, mediating the dialogue between hand and material.

As the form emerges, the conversation deepens. We begin to see the subtleties of the stone's character revealed in the play of light and shadow across its surface. The veining, once a random pattern, becomes an integral part of the composition, adding depth and complexity. A flaw, initially perceived as an imperfection, might transform into a unique feature, a testament to the stone's individual history. These serendipitous discoveries are gifts from the material, unexpected turns in the ongoing dialogue. They enrich the work, imbuing it with a sense of authenticity and life.

The final stages of the process are a refinement of this dialogue. We work with increasingly finer tools, polishing the surface to bring out the stone's inherent luminosity. This final touch is not merely cosmetic. It's an act of reverence, a way of honoring the material and the journey we have taken together. It's a recognition that the true beauty of the sculpture lies not in its perfect form, but in the dialogue between the artist and the material, the story of their shared creation. The finished piece stands as a testament to this intimate exchange, a tangible record of the conversation between stone and spirit. It whispers of the sculptor's vision, but also of the stone's inherent character, its history, its essence. It's a silent dialogue made visible, a tangible expression of the creative process, a testament to the transformative power of listening to the voice of matter. This understanding, this deep respect for the material, is the foundation of all sculptural creation. It's the key to unlocking the potential that lies within each block of stone, waiting to be revealed through the hands of the sculptor. The conversation doesn't end with the completion of the work. It continues in the viewer's experience, in the way they perceive and interpret the form, the texture, the light. The sculpture becomes a conduit for a new dialogue, a conversation that extends across time and space, connecting artist, material, and observer in a shared experience of beauty and meaning. This ongoing exchange is the essence of art, its enduring power to connect us to the world and to each other. The dialogue, in its many forms, continues.

The act of sculpting, then, is not a conquest of matter, but a collaboration with it. It is a process of listening, of responding, of allowing the material to speak. The sculptor's hand is guided not only by vision but also by the inherent qualities of the stone, its weight, its texture, its internal structure. The finished sculpture is not simply an object, but a record of this dialogue, a tangible expression of the interplay between human intention and the material world.

2 Chapter 2: Memory in Marble

Marble, in its cool, translucent depths, holds a unique capacity for capturing memory. Not in the way of a photograph, freezing a fleeting instant, but rather as a vessel for emotional resonance, a whisper of past sensations. Think of the subtle veining, like the tracery of veins beneath skin, each a unique map of time and pressure. These patterns, formed over millennia, hold within them the echoes of geological upheavals, the slow, inexorable drift of continents. When I work with marble, I feel a connection not just to the material itself, but to the vast expanse of time it represents.

Consider the way light penetrates the stone, revealing a soft, inner glow. This luminosity speaks to the interplay of presence and absence, a tangible reminder of the ephemeral nature of experience. A sculpted form in marble can capture the essence of a moment, not through literal representation, but through the evocation of feeling. A curve can suggest the gentle slope of a shoulder, a polished plane the smoothness of skin. The memory resides not in the precise replication of form, but in the resonance of the material itself. It is a dialogue between the stone's inherent qualities and the sculptor's intention, a dance between the tangible and intangible.

My own experiences find their way into the marble, shaping the forms that emerge. The memory of a childhood spent exploring the rugged coastline near my home, the rhythmic crash of waves against the shore, the feel of salt-laced wind on my face—these sensations inform the curves and hollows I carve. They are not literal depictions of the sea, but rather echoes of its power and tranquility, distilled into the stone. The coolness of the marble reminds me of the smooth, wet stones I collected as a child, each one a small treasure held in my palm. This tactile memory, embedded deep within me, finds its expression in the polished surfaces of my sculptures.

The process of sculpting is itself a form of remembering. The rhythmic tapping of the chisel, the rasp of the file against the stone—these actions create a physical connection to the material, a dialogue that transcends words. Each strike of the chisel releases a fine dust, a tangible reminder of the transformation taking place. As the form emerges from the block, it becomes imbued with the energy of the process, a physical manifestation of the sculptor's intention and memory. This embodied memory resonates within the finished piece, inviting the viewer to engage with it on a deeper level.

Marble's inherent translucence also plays a crucial role in this interplay of memory and material. The way light filters through the stone, creating subtle variations in tone and depth, can evoke a sense of ethereal beauty, a whisper of something beyond the purely physical. This quality allows for the creation of forms that seem to hover between presence and absence, capturing the fleeting nature of memory itself. It's a reminder that memories, like light, are constantly shifting and changing, shaped by time and perspective. They are not static entities, but rather fluid and dynamic forces that shape our understanding of the world.

The very act of carving into marble is an act of preservation, a way of freezing a moment in time. Yet, paradoxically, it is also an acknowledgment of the ephemeral nature of existence. The stone, though seemingly permanent, is subject to the slow but relentless forces of erosion and decay. This awareness of impermanence adds another layer of meaning to the work, reminding us to cherish the present moment and the memories that shape our lives. The sculpted form becomes a testament to the fleeting beauty of existence, a tangible reminder of the preciousness of time.

Finally, consider the role of the viewer in this interplay of memory and material. Each individual brings their own experiences and interpretations to the encounter with the sculpture. The curves and hollows, the polished surfaces, and the play of light and shadow evoke different memories and emotions in each observer. The sculpture becomes a catalyst for personal reflection, a mirror reflecting the viewer's own inner landscape. In this way, the memory embedded within the marble expands beyond the personal experience of the sculptor to encompass a shared human experience, a testament to the power of art to connect us to each other and to the world around us.

2.1 Frozen Moments

Consider the act of sculpting not just as forming the stone, but as revealing what already lies within. Think of a block of marble, seemingly inert, yet holding the potential for a human form, a bird in flight, an abstract emotion. Memory resides not only in our minds but also in the world around us, embedded in the very fabric of existence. Marble, with its delicate veins and subtle variations in color, serves as a particularly potent vessel for these captured moments. Each fissure, each crystalline inclusion, whispers tales of geological time, of pressures and transformations that shaped the stone long before it met the sculptor's hand. We, as artists, intercept these narratives, weaving them into our own expressions of memory and experience.

Imagine carving a portrait. You're not merely replicating the outward appearance, but striving to capture a fleeting expression, a glimmer in the eye that reveals a personality, a history. That precise moment, frozen in time, becomes your guiding principle. The curve of a lip, the furrow of a brow – these details transcend mere representation; they become imbued with the emotional weight of the memory they embody. The coldness of the stone belies the warmth of human experience it comes to hold.

This concept extends beyond the human form. Consider a still life sculpted in marble – a draped cloth, a bowl of fruit. Even these seemingly mundane objects can evoke a flood of associations. The folds of the fabric might recall a loved one's garment, the ripeness of the fruit a specific moment of shared pleasure. By imbuing these objects with the weight of personal experience, the sculptor transforms them from mere representations into potent symbols of memory. The stone, in its immutability, becomes a paradoxical vessel for the ephemeral nature of time and experience.

Think of the way light plays across a polished marble surface, revealing the subtle nuances of its form. The interplay of light and shadow evokes a sense of movement, even within the stillness of the stone. This dynamism adds another layer to the concept of frozen moments, suggesting that memory itself is not static but a fluid and evolving entity. The sculpture becomes a stage for this interplay, inviting the viewer to engage with the captured moment from multiple perspectives.

Furthermore, the act of carving itself becomes a form of remembering. The physical process of chipping away at the stone, of shaping its contours, is a deeply meditative act. It's a dialogue with the material, a slow and deliberate uncovering of the form within. In this process, the sculptor's own memories and experiences inevitably surface, influencing the direction of the work. The rhythm of the chisel against the stone becomes a rhythm of recollection, a tangible connection to the past.

Reflect on the permanence of stone. Unlike more ephemeral materials, marble offers a sense of enduring presence. This permanence contributes to the power of sculpted memories. The frozen moment, captured in stone, transcends the limitations of human lifespan. It becomes a testament to the enduring power of experience, a tangible link to the past that can be shared across generations. The solidity of the material reinforces the significance of the memory it holds, giving it a weight and gravity that resonates with the viewer.

Consider the inherent beauty of marble itself. Its translucence, its smooth texture, these qualities contribute to the evocative power of the sculpture. The material itself becomes a metaphor for the fragility and preciousness of memory. The delicate veins and subtle variations in color add depth and complexity to the captured moment, hinting at the layers of meaning embedded within. This interplay between material and meaning elevates the sculpture beyond mere representation, transforming it into a powerful meditation on time, memory, and human experience. The artist, through the act of sculpting, breathes life into the stone, imbuing it with a spirit that speaks to us across the ages. In the frozen moment, we find a reflection of ourselves, a connection to the past, and a glimpse into the enduring power of human experience etched in stone.

2.2 Echoes in the Grain

The veined intricacies within a block of marble often whisper narratives of bygone eras. Consider the geological processes, the immense pressures and the slow, inexorable shifts that formed the very substance we sculpt. These forces leave their indelible mark, a language of texture and pattern etched into the stone's heart. When I approach a new piece, I run my hands across its surface, seeking to decipher these silent stories, allowing them to inform and inspire the emerging form. It's a conversation across millennia, a communion with the earth's ancient memory. Each fissure, each subtle shift in coloration, becomes a potential pathway for the narrative to unfold. This inherent memory held within the stone isn't limited to geological time. Think about the human touch, the tools that have quarried and shaped the block throughout history. Each swing of the pickaxe, each carefully placed chisel mark, leaves an energetic residue, a ghostly echo of past labors. These traces, often invisible to the naked eye, contribute to the overall character of the stone, imbuing it with a palpable sense of history. When we carve, we are adding our own layer to this complex palimpsest, continuing the ongoing dialogue between human intention and the material world. We become part of the stone's story, and it, in turn, becomes part of ours.

For me, this connection to the past is most potent when working with salvaged marble. Pieces reclaimed from demolished buildings, discarded fragments of architectural ornamentation – these carry within them the weight of human experience in a particularly poignant way. Imagine a marble lintel, once gracing the entrance to a grand estate, now fractured and worn, yet still retaining the faintest hint of its former elegance. To carve into such a piece is to engage not just with the stone itself, but also with the lives that once brushed against it, the stories that unfolded beneath its shadow. The sculpture becomes a vessel for these accumulated memories, transformed and recontextualized within a new narrative.

This interplay between the past and the present, between the stone's inherent memory and the sculptor's intention, is at the heart of my practice. It's a delicate dance, a constant negotiation between honoring the existing narrative and imposing my own vision. I often find myself working intuitively, allowing the grain and texture of the marble to guide my hand, to suggest the form that lies dormant within. There are moments when the chisel seems to move of its own accord, as if guided by the whispers of the stone itself. It's in these moments of surrender, when I relinquish complete control, that the most compelling work emerges.

Consider the role of light and shadow in revealing these embedded narratives. The way light plays across a polished surface, highlighting the subtle variations in color and texture, can evoke a sense of depth and mystery. A carefully placed shadow can accentuate a particular curve or crevice, drawing the viewer's eye to a specific detail, whispering a secret only they can decipher. The interplay of light and shadow becomes another layer of storytelling, adding another dimension to the sculpture's expressive potential. It's a subtle language, but one that speaks directly to our subconscious, evoking emotions and associations that lie just beneath the surface of our awareness.

This process of uncovering and amplifying the inherent narratives within the stone is not simply about recreating the past. It's about transforming it, imbuing it with new meaning and relevance. By engaging with the stone's memory, we can create works that resonate with a depth and complexity that goes beyond mere aesthetics. The sculpture becomes a bridge between the past and the present, a tangible link to the ongoing flow of time. It's a reminder that we are all part of a larger narrative, a continuum of human experience etched into the very fabric of the world around us. And through the act of sculpting, we can become active participants in this unfolding story, shaping not only the stone, but also our own understanding of our place within the grand tapestry of existence. The sculptor's hand, guided by the whispers of the stone, becomes a conduit for memory, transforming the raw material of the earth into a vessel of enduring meaning. It's a transformative act, a testament to the power of human creativity to engage with the deepest layers of time and experience.

3 Chapter 3: The Spirit of Place

A sculptor doesn't just choose a stone; they engage with a piece of the earth. This engagement extends beyond the physical act of carving. It encompasses an understanding of the stone's origin, the forces that shaped it, and the environment it inhabited for millennia. Consider a block of granite quarried from a mountainside. It carries within it the weight of that mountain, the memory of glacial ice, the slow, persistent pressure of tectonic plates. To sculpt this granite is to tap into that history, to become a part of its ongoing narrative. The final artwork, then, becomes more than just an object; it becomes a vessel containing the spirit of place.

The connection between stone and place manifests in various ways. Sometimes, it's a direct representation of the landscape. A sculptor might carve the sweeping curves of a desert canyon into sandstone, capturing the essence of that specific environment. Other times, the connection is more subtle, expressed through texture, form, and the interplay of light and shadow. A piece of polished basalt, mirroring the dark sheen of a volcanic rock face, can evoke a powerful sense of place without explicitly depicting it. The sculptor acts as a translator, interpreting the language of the land and conveying its essence through the medium of stone.

This intimate relationship with place informs every stage of the creative process. The choice of stone, the sculpting techniques employed, and the final placement of the artwork are all influenced by the sculptor's understanding of the environment. For example, a sculpture intended for a coastal setting might be carved from a weather-resistant stone like granite, its rough texture echoing the rugged coastline. The forms themselves might be shaped to complement the movement of the wind and waves, creating a harmonious dialogue between art and nature. Conversely, a sculpture destined for a tranquil garden might be carved from a softer, more delicate stone like alabaster, its smooth surface reflecting the serenity of the surroundings.

The act of placing the sculpture within its chosen environment completes the connection. A sculpture situated in a public park becomes a focal point, inviting interaction and contemplation. Its presence alters the dynamics of the space, transforming a simple patch of grass into a place of meaning and reflection. Similarly, a sculpture nestled within a private garden becomes an integral part of the landscape, offering a sense of sanctuary and personal connection. The sculpture anchors itself to the earth, becoming rooted in its new home.

This sense of belonging extends beyond the physical placement of the sculpture. It resonates with the viewer on an emotional and spiritual level. When we encounter a sculpture that is deeply connected to its place, we experience a sense of harmony and resonance. We feel a kinship with the land, a deeper understanding of our own place within the world. The sculpture acts as a conduit, connecting us to the spirit of the place and enriching our experience of it.

Consider the ancient standing stones of prehistoric cultures. These monolithic structures, often placed in alignment with celestial bodies or natural landmarks, served as powerful symbols of place and belonging. They marked sacred sites, defined territories, and connected communities to the rhythms of the earth. In a similar way, contemporary sculptures can evoke a sense of reverence and connection to the environment.

Ultimately, the spirit of place embodied in a sculpture transcends the purely material. It becomes a reflection of our relationship with the natural world, a testament to the enduring power of art to connect us to something larger than ourselves. It reminds us that we are not separate from nature, but rather an integral part of its intricate tapestry. The sculptor, through their intimate understanding of stone and place, invites us to share in this profound connection and to find sanctuary within the beauty of the earth.

3.1 Landscapes Within

The human experience is inextricably linked to place. We are shaped by the landscapes we inhabit, the contours of the land imprinting themselves upon our memories and emotions. As sculptors, we carry these internal landscapes within us, and they inevitably find expression in our work. This chapter explores the ways in which our inner geographies—those deeply personal, emotional, and psychological terrains—emerge through the act of sculpting. Consider the sheer cliffs of Dover, etched white against the blue expanse of the English Channel. Their stark beauty might evoke a sense of awe, perhaps even a touch of vulnerability in the face of nature's grandeur. A sculptor might translate this feeling into the sharp, angular planes of a marble form, conveying the cliff's imposing presence and the emotional response it provokes. The smooth, cool surface of the stone could further enhance the sensation of windswept exposure, creating a tactile dialogue with the viewer.

This connection between internal landscape and external form isn't always so literal. It's not about simply replicating a physical location in stone. Instead, it's about capturing the essence of a place, its emotional resonance, and translating it into a three-dimensional language. Think of the rolling hills of Tuscany, bathed in the golden light of a late afternoon sun. A sculptor might not carve a miniature replica of this scene. Rather, they might evoke its gentle curves and warm hues through the subtle modulation of a form, creating a sense of tranquility and harmony that mirrors the landscape's effect on the soul. The material itself can play a crucial role in this translation. A rough-hewn granite, for example, might be chosen to represent the rugged terrain of a mountain range, while a polished alabaster could express the serenity of a moonlit desert.

The process of uncovering these internal landscapes is often intuitive. We might begin with a vague sense of unease, a yearning for a particular emotional tone, or a fragmented memory of a place we once knew. As we work with the stone, these internal sensations begin to take shape. The act of chipping away at the material, of revealing the form within, becomes a process of self-discovery. Each strike of the chisel brings us closer to understanding the emotional terrain we're exploring. Imagine the desolate expanse of the Arctic tundra, its vastness stretching towards a horizon shrouded in mist. The sculptor might translate this sense of isolation and mystery through the creation of a solitary, elongated form, its surface etched with the traces of time and weathering, echoing the unforgiving nature of the environment. The negative space surrounding the sculpture could further amplify this feeling of emptiness and solitude.

Our internal landscapes are not static. They shift and evolve with our experiences, just as the external world is constantly changing. A childhood memory of a sun-drenched beach can be overlaid with the melancholy of loss as we grow older. A bustling city street, once experienced as a place of excitement and opportunity, might later evoke feelings of alienation and anonymity. These complexities are embedded within our artistic expression, adding layers of meaning to the forms we create. Consider the intricate network of canals in Venice, their shimmering surfaces reflecting the city's rich history and vibrant culture. A sculptor might capture this sense of fluidity and interconnectedness through a series of interwoven forms, their polished surfaces reflecting light and shadow, evoking the interplay of water and architecture. The use of contrasting textures could further represent the city's diverse population and its multifaceted character.

Ultimately, the landscapes within are as diverse and unique as the individuals who create them. They are a testament to the profound connection between our inner lives and the external world, a testament to the power of art to give tangible form to the intangible. By exploring these internal geographies, we not only deepen our understanding of ourselves but also offer a glimpse into the shared human experience of place, memory, and emotion. The stone becomes a conduit, a bridge between our inner and outer worlds, allowing us to communicate the ineffable through the language of form. This dialogue between stone and spirit, between material and memory, is at the heart of the sculptor's craft. It is a journey of exploration, a process of discovery that reveals not only the landscapes within but also the profound interconnectedness of all things. Through the act of sculpting, we carve out a space for ourselves in the world, leaving behind a tangible expression of our inner being, a testament to the enduring power of human creativity.

3.2 Stone and Setting

Consider the profound impact of setting on a sculpture. A figure carved from rough granite, placed in a bustling city square, resonates differently than the same figure nestled within a quiet forest glade. The urban setting might amplify the sculpture's strength, its resilience against the relentless energy of human activity. The natural setting, conversely, might invite contemplation, encouraging a dialogue between the stone and the whispering leaves, the dappled sunlight filtering through the canopy. The setting becomes an integral part of the artwork, a silent partner in its conversation with the world.

Think of the specific qualities of a location that can enhance or diminish a sculpture's presence. A coastal setting, with its salt-laced air and the rhythmic pulse of the tides, might call for a material that can weather the elements, a stone with a texture that echoes the roughness of the sea-worn cliffs. A formal garden, meticulously planned and manicured, might provide a backdrop for a more polished, refined piece, perhaps a marble figure whose smooth contours complement the ordered beauty of its surroundings. The interplay between the sculpture and its environment creates a dynamic relationship, a subtle tension that adds depth and meaning to the artwork.

The scale of the setting is equally crucial. A monumental sculpture placed in a vast open space can evoke a sense of awe, its size emphasizing the grandeur of the landscape. Imagine a towering abstract form against the backdrop of a desert canyon, its stark silhouette mirroring the jagged peaks. The same sculpture in a confined space would lose its impact, its power dwarfed by the close proximity of walls or other structures. Conversely, a smaller, more intimate piece might be lost in a vast setting, its delicate details overlooked in the immensity of its surroundings. The sculptor must carefully consider the scale of both the sculpture and the setting to achieve a harmonious balance.

Orientation also plays a significant role. How a sculpture is positioned in relation to the sun, the prevailing winds, or the surrounding vegetation can dramatically affect its appearance and perceived meaning. A figure facing the rising sun might symbolize hope and renewal, while the same figure turned towards the setting sun might evoke a sense of melancholy or reflection. A sculpture placed amidst a grove of trees might appear to emerge organically from the natural world, while one standing alone on a barren plain might convey a sense of isolation or defiance. The sculptor's careful consideration of these elements allows the setting to become an active participant in the narrative of the artwork.

Beyond the physical attributes of the setting, consider its historical and cultural context. A sculpture placed in a location with a rich history can acquire layers of meaning, resonating with the stories and memories embedded in the place. Imagine a contemporary sculpture installed in the ruins of an ancient temple, the juxtaposition of old and new creating a powerful dialogue across time. Similarly, a sculpture placed in a community with a strong artistic tradition can become part of a larger cultural conversation, enriching the community's sense of identity and place.

Finally, contemplate the intended interaction between the viewer and the sculpture within its chosen setting. Does the setting invite contemplation or interaction? A sculpture placed in a public park might encourage viewers to touch it, to walk around it, to experience it from different perspectives. A sculpture displayed in a museum setting, on the other hand, might necessitate a more detached, observational approach. The setting influences not only how the sculpture is perceived but also how the viewer engages with it, shaping the overall experience of the artwork. By thoughtfully considering these elements, the sculptor transforms the setting from a mere backdrop into an essential component of the sculpture's expressive power. The setting becomes a canvas upon which the artwork is painted, a stage upon which its story unfolds. It is in this careful interplay between stone, setting, and spirit that the sculpture truly comes alive.

3.3 A Sense of Belonging

The act of creating, of shaping stone into a form that resonates with the human spirit, is intrinsically linked to a sense of place. This connection transcends mere geographical location; it delves into the profound interplay between the artist, the material, and the environment in which the creation takes place. Consider the quarry, the source of the stone itself. It is a place of extraction, a wound in the earth, yet also a place of potential, where raw material awaits transformation. The sculptor's studio, too, becomes a locus of creative energy, a space imbued with the dust of past endeavors and the anticipation of future forms. These places, both natural and constructed, become integral to the artwork's narrative, whispering their stories into the very grain of the stone.

This sense of place extends beyond the physical locations involved in the creation process. The surrounding landscape, the quality of light, the prevailing winds—all contribute to the sculptor's vision. A sculpture conceived in the harsh light of the desert will differ markedly from one born amidst the lush greenery of a forest. The environment imprints itself upon the artist's consciousness, subtly shaping their aesthetic choices and informing the final form of the work. Think of the ancient stone circles, their placement carefully aligned with celestial events, their forms echoing the surrounding hills. These works become inextricably linked to their environment, serving as focal points for human interaction with the natural world.

Furthermore, the placement of a finished sculpture is crucial to its meaning. A monumental figure placed in a bustling city square will evoke a different response than the same figure nestled within a contemplative garden. The surrounding context influences how the viewer perceives the work, adding layers of interpretation and meaning. The sculpture becomes part of the fabric of the place, contributing to its identity and enriching the experience of those who encounter it. Consider the weathered gargoyles perched atop ancient cathedrals, their forms both protective and ominous, their presence inextricably linked to the sacred space they inhabit.

This sense of belonging goes beyond the relationship between the sculpture and its immediate surroundings. It encompasses a broader connection to the cultural and historical context in which the work is created. A sculptor working within a specific tradition, whether it be classical, modern, or indigenous, carries the weight of that tradition within their practice. Their work becomes a continuation of a lineage, a dialogue with the past that informs the present and shapes the future. Think of the intricate carvings on totem poles, each symbol imbued with generations of stories and cultural significance.

Ultimately, this sense of belonging fostered through the creation and placement of sculpture reflects a fundamental human desire for connection. We seek to root ourselves in the world, to leave our mark upon the landscape, to create spaces of meaning and resonance. Stone, with its inherent permanence, offers a powerful medium for expressing this desire. Through the sculptor's hand, the inert material is transformed into a vessel of memory, a testament to the enduring human spirit, and a tangible link to the places that shape our lives. The sculpture becomes a bridge between the material and the immaterial, the tangible and the intangible, connecting us to the earth, to history, and to each other. This deep connection imbues the work with a power that transcends mere aesthetics, transforming it into a source of solace, inspiration, and a profound sense of belonging. It is in these moments of connection, when the stone speaks and the spirit listens, that the true power of sculpture is revealed. This profound interplay between the material and the immaterial underscores the importance of place in shaping not only the artwork itself but also

our experience of it. The sculpture becomes a conduit, connecting us to the earth, to history, and to the enduring human spirit.
The sculptor's journey is one of constant exploration, a continuous dialogue with the material and the environment. This dialogue extends beyond the physical act of shaping stone, encompassing a deeper engagement with the cultural and historical context in which the work is created. The sculptor's hand, guided by both intuition and skill, translates this dialogue into tangible form, imbuing the stone with meaning and purpose. The resulting sculpture stands as a testament to this intricate interplay of forces, a tangible manifestation of the artist's connection to place. It serves as a reminder of our own interconnectedness with the world around us, inviting us to pause, reflect, and find our own sense of belonging within the vast tapestry of existence. This is the power of sculpture: to connect us to something larger than ourselves, to ground us in the present moment, and to offer a glimpse into the timeless beauty of the natural world. It is through this connection that we find meaning, not only in the artwork itself but also in our own lives and our place within the grand scheme of things.

3.4 Rooted in Earth

The earth breathes beneath our feet, a constant, silent presence that anchors us to this world. It offers not just physical grounding but a deep connection to the cyclical nature of existence, the slow, steady rhythm of growth and decay, creation and erosion. As sculptors, we engage with this elemental force, drawing inspiration from the land itself, its contours and textures, its hidden stories whispered on the wind. This connection grounds our work, infusing it with a sense of place and belonging that transcends the purely aesthetic. Consider the geological history embedded within each stone, the millennia of pressure and transformation that have shaped its very being. This history becomes part of the sculpture's narrative, adding layers of meaning that resonate with the viewer on a visceral level.

This inherent energy of the earth, palpable in the raw materials we work with, informs every stage of the creative process. From the initial selection of a stone to the final placement of the finished piece, we are guided by a sense of reverence for the land and its gifts. The very act of quarrying, of extracting stone from the earth, is a powerful reminder of our interconnectedness with the natural world. It is an act that demands respect, a recognition that we are borrowing from the earth, not taking from it. We become participants in a continuous dialogue with the landscape, a conversation that stretches back through time and connects us to generations of artists who have sought inspiration in the same source. The sculptor's studio becomes a microcosm of this larger exchange, a place where the earth's energy is harnessed and transformed into tangible form.

The specific location of creation significantly influences the final artwork. A coastal studio, exposed to the relentless power of the sea, might inspire works that reflect the fluidity and dynamism of water. A studio nestled in the mountains, surrounded by towering peaks and ancient forests, might evoke a sense of stillness and contemplation. The subtle shifts in light, the prevailing winds, the sounds of the natural world—all these elements seep into the creative process, shaping the form and texture of the sculpture. The environment becomes a collaborator, whispering its secrets into the artist's ear.

The choice of stone itself reflects this intimate relationship with place. Local stone, quarried from the surrounding landscape, carries within it the unique geological fingerprint of that region. Its color, texture, and even its scent are imbued with the spirit of the place. Using local stone creates a tangible link between the artwork and its environment, strengthening the sense of belonging and rootedness. It's a testament to the power of place to shape not only our physical surroundings but also our artistic vision. This specificity imbues the work with a sense of authenticity, a direct connection to the source of its inspiration.

Consider the placement of the finished sculpture. Will it stand alone in a gallery, or will it be integrated into the landscape, becoming part of the natural environment? A sculpture placed outdoors, exposed to the elements, will weather and change over time, developing a patina that reflects its ongoing dialogue with the earth. This natural transformation becomes part of the artwork's story, a testament to the cyclical nature of existence. Even indoors, the placement of a sculpture can evoke a sense of place, creating a focal point that anchors the surrounding space. The sculpture becomes a conduit between the viewer and the earth, inviting contemplation and connection.

By embracing the earth as both material and inspiration, we create sculptures that resonate with a deeper meaning. These works become more than just objects; they become vessels of memory, reflections on time, and expressions of our profound connection to the natural world. They speak a language that transcends words, a language rooted in the very earth that sustains us. This grounding, this deep connection to place, is what gives our work its power and enduring presence. It allows us to create art that not only speaks to the present but also whispers to the future, carrying the echoes of the earth's ancient story. This intimate dialogue with the material, with the earth itself, is the essence of what it means to be a sculptor.

3.5 Finding Sanctuary

Sanctuary isn't solely found in grand cathedrals or remote mountaintops. It exists in the subtle curve of a coastline, the weathered face of a cliff, the quiet strength of a single, perfectly placed stone. For the sculptor, finding sanctuary often means recognizing the inherent power of place and allowing it to permeate the creative process. It's about understanding how a sculpture can not only inhabit a space but also enhance and become an integral part of its environment. This understanding transforms the act of creation into a conversation with the surrounding world. We don't simply impose our will upon the stone; we listen to the whispers of the wind, the rhythm of the waves, the stillness of the earth, and allow these elements to inform our work.

Consider the placement of ancient megaliths, positioned with astronomical precision, their rough surfaces mirroring the contours of the land. These structures weren't simply dropped onto the landscape; they emerged from it, a testament to the deep connection between human creativity and the natural world. Think of the way a weathered statue in a garden, softened by moss and rain, becomes a focal point for contemplation, a place where the boundary between art and nature blurs. This integration, this harmonious blending, is key to understanding the concept of sanctuary in sculpture. It requires a sensitivity to the subtle nuances of the environment and a willingness to let the spirit of place guide the creative hand.

This connection goes beyond mere aesthetics. It speaks to a fundamental human need to find our place within the larger tapestry of existence. We seek spaces that resonate with our inner selves, places where we feel grounded, connected, and at peace. Sculpture, when thoughtfully integrated into its environment, can create such spaces. A carefully placed piece can draw our attention to the beauty of a hidden alcove, frame a breathtaking vista, or invite us to pause and reflect amidst the bustling activity of a city square. The sculpture becomes a conduit, connecting us to the spirit of the place and, in turn, to ourselves.

The process of finding sanctuary through sculpture begins with observation. Spend time in the intended location. Absorb its atmosphere. Feel the texture of the earth beneath your feet. Notice the patterns of light and shadow. Listen to the sounds that fill the air.

Allow the essence of the place to seep into your consciousness. This immersive experience will inform your artistic choices, guiding the selection of material, the shape of the form, and its ultimate placement. A sculpture intended for a windswept coastal setting will likely differ dramatically from one designed for a tranquil forest glade.

Choosing the right stone is paramount. Each type of stone possesses its own unique character and energy. A rough-hewn granite boulder might convey a sense of permanence and strength, while a smooth piece of alabaster could evoke a feeling of fragility and ethereal beauty. The color and texture of the stone also play a significant role in how a sculpture interacts with its surroundings. A dark, polished stone might absorb the light, creating a sense of mystery, while a light, textured stone might reflect the sunlight, adding a touch of vibrancy to the space. Consider the relationship between the stone's inherent qualities and the prevailing atmosphere of the place.

The form of the sculpture should also be in dialogue with its environment. A soaring, vertical piece might emphasize the height of a towering cliff, while a low, horizontal form could echo the gentle curve of a hillside. The interplay of lines, curves, and voids can create a dynamic tension or a sense of quiet repose, depending on the desired effect. The goal is to create a harmonious relationship between the sculpture and its surroundings, so that each enhances the other.

Finally, the placement of the sculpture is crucial. A carefully chosen location can transform a simple piece of stone into a powerful focal point, a place of contemplation, a sanctuary. Consider the path of the sun, the direction of the wind, the natural flow of movement through the space. Think about how the sculpture will interact with the existing elements – the trees, the rocks, the water. The ideal placement will allow the sculpture to become an integral part of the environment, enhancing its natural beauty and creating a sense of peace and harmony.

Finding sanctuary through sculpture is a journey of discovery, a process of connecting with both the inner and outer landscapes. It is a testament to the transformative power of art and its ability to create spaces of meaning and resonance. It is a reminder that true sanctuary is not found in escaping the world, but in finding our place within it.

4 Chapter 4: Tools and Techniques

The sculptor's studio, a space of dust and potential, echoes with the ring of hammer against chisel. Within this creative sanctuary, a transformation occurs. Raw, unyielding stone gradually surrenders to the artist's vision, revealing the form slumbering within. This metamorphosis is not achieved through brute force alone, but through a delicate dance between the sculptor's intention and the tools that extend their will. Understanding this intimate relationship between artist and instrument is paramount.

Consider the point chisel, a slender tool of hardened steel, its tip forged to a precise point. This seemingly simple instrument is capable of both delicate detail and aggressive removal. With a controlled tap, it can delineate a sharp line, separating plane from plane. Driven with greater force, it can carve deep into the stone, excavating mass and revealing underlying structure. Mastering the point chisel requires not only physical dexterity but also a sensitivity to the stone's resistance, an understanding of its inherent grain and texture. This tactile dialogue informs the sculptor's every move, guiding the chisel's dance across the stone's surface.

The toothed chisel, or claw chisel, presents a different approach. Its multiple teeth, like miniature wedges, bite into the stone, removing material in a series of controlled fractures. This tool excels at roughing out forms, quickly reducing large masses of stone to manageable proportions. Its rhythmic percussion fills the studio with a percussive energy, a testament to the sculptor's physical engagement with the material. However, finesse is still required. The angle of the chisel, the force of the blow, these subtle variations determine the texture and character of the sculpted surface. Too aggressive an approach can lead to unwanted breakage, a stark reminder of the stone's inherent fragility.

Beyond these primary chisels, a vast array of specialized tools await the sculptor's hand. The flat chisel, with its broad blade, smooths and refines surfaces, creating planes of exquisite subtlety. The rondel, a curved chisel, carves concave forms, adding depth and dimension to the emerging sculpture. Each tool possesses a unique voice, a specific capacity for shaping the stone. The sculptor, like a conductor leading an orchestra, must understand and orchestrate these diverse voices, harmonizing their individual contributions to create a unified whole.

But tools alone are insufficient. Technique, the learned skill of wielding these instruments, is essential. The sculptor's grip, the stance, the swing of the hammer, all contribute to the final outcome. Proper technique maximizes efficiency, allowing the sculptor to work with precision and control. It also minimizes the risk of injury, protecting both the artist and the artwork. Years of practice are required to develop this embodied knowledge, to internalize the subtle movements that transform raw material into artistic expression.

Consider the process of "pointing," a fundamental technique used to transfer a three-dimensional design from a clay maquette to the stone block. This meticulous process involves carefully measuring points on the maquette and transferring those measurements to the stone using a pointing machine. Precision is paramount. Even the slightest deviation can distort the final form. The sculptor's patient hand and keen eye guide the process, ensuring that the essence of the original design is faithfully translated into stone.

Another crucial technique is "pitching," the controlled removal of large sections of stone. This involves using a pitching tool, a heavy chisel with a wide blade, to create deep, angled cuts that define the overall shape of the sculpture. This stage requires both strength and precision. The sculptor must anticipate how the stone will fracture, carefully directing the force of each blow to avoid unwanted breakage. The process is a delicate balance between aggression and control, a testament to the sculptor's deep understanding of the material's properties.

Beyond these fundamental techniques, a myriad of specialized methods exist, each tailored to specific materials and artistic goals. Bush hammering, for instance, creates a textured surface by repeatedly striking the stone with a textured hammer. Abrasive techniques, using sandpaper or other abrasive materials, refine and polish the surface, revealing the stone's inherent beauty. The sculptor's repertoire of techniques expands over time, evolving alongside their artistic vision.

The sculptor's relationship with tools and techniques extends beyond mere practicality. It's a deep connection, an intimate dialogue between artist and material. The tools become extensions of the sculptor's hand, translating thought and emotion into tangible form. The techniques, honed through years of practice, become a language, a means of communicating with the stone. Through this constant interplay, the sculptor shapes not only the material but also their own understanding of the creative process. They shape the void, transforming absence into presence, silence into story. And within that transformation, they find their own unique voice.

4.1 The Sculptor's Hand

The sculptor's hand is more than merely a tool; it is a conduit, a translator of inner vision into tangible form. It is through the hand that the cold, inert mass of stone is awakened, imbued with life and meaning. This transformation is not achieved through brute force, but rather through a nuanced understanding of the material and a delicate interplay of pressure and precision. Consider the subtle shift in grip as the sculptor assesses the stone's resistance, the gentle caress that reveals the hidden grain, the decisive strike that removes excess material. These actions, seemingly small, are the vocabulary of a conversation between artist and material, a dialogue whispered across the centuries.

Understanding the properties of your chosen stone is paramount. A sculptor working with granite approaches the material differently than one working with alabaster. The density, texture, and even the color of the stone inform the artist's approach. A hard, crystalline stone like granite demands controlled, deliberate actions, each chisel mark a testament to patience and precision. Softer stones like alabaster allow for a more fluid, expressive touch, inviting the sculptor to explore subtle nuances of form and texture. This intimate knowledge of the material is not acquired overnight; it is earned through years of dedicated practice, through countless hours of hands-on experience, of feeling the stone's response beneath the fingertips.

The tools themselves are extensions of the sculptor's hand, each designed for a specific purpose. The point chisel, with its sharp, focused tip, is used for fine detailing and intricate carving. The tooth chisel, with its multiple cutting edges, removes larger portions of stone, rapidly shaping the overall form. The claw chisel, resembling a miniature rake, is employed for texturing and refining surfaces. Beyond these basic tools, a sculptor's arsenal may include a wide array of specialized chisels, hammers, rasps, and rifflers, each chosen for its unique ability to shape and refine the stone. The selection and use of these tools are not merely technical matters; they are deeply intertwined with the artist's creative intent. The rhythmic clang of the hammer against the chisel, the rasping sound of a file smoothing the surface – these are the sounds of creation, the soundtrack of the sculptor's journey.

Beyond the physical act of carving, the sculptor's hand also plays a crucial role in the conceptualization of the work. Before the first chisel touches the stone, the sculptor's hands are already at work, sketching, molding clay maquettes, exploring the potential forms that reside within the raw material. This tactile exploration allows the artist to internalize the three-dimensional nature of the sculpture, to anticipate the challenges and opportunities that will arise during the carving process. It is in these early stages, through the manipulation of clay or plaster, that the initial spark of inspiration is nurtured and transformed into a concrete vision.

The connection between hand and mind is essential in sculpture. The hand acts as a feedback mechanism, constantly informing the brain about the stone's resistance, its texture, its temperature. This constant flow of information allows the sculptor to make subtle adjustments in technique, to respond to the unique characteristics of each individual piece of stone. This interplay between hand and mind is not a purely conscious process; it is often intuitive, almost instinctive. Years of practice imbue the sculptor's hands with a kind of intelligence, a sensitivity that allows them to "read" the stone and respond accordingly.

The act of sculpting is not simply about removing material; it is also about shaping the void, creating negative spaces that interact with the positive forms to define the overall composition. The interplay of light and shadow within these negative spaces can add depth, drama, and even a sense of movement to the sculpture. A skilled sculptor understands the power of the void, using it to enhance the expressive qualities of the work, to draw the viewer's eye and evoke a range of emotions.

Ultimately, the sculptor's hand is a testament to the power of human creativity. It is a reminder that even the most seemingly intractable materials can be transformed through dedication, skill, and a deep understanding of the creative process. The finished sculpture stands as a testament to this transformative power, a tangible embodiment of the artist's vision, brought to life through the skilled and sensitive touch of the sculptor's hand. The process is a meditation, a physical and spiritual engagement with the material world. The hand becomes the bridge between the intangible realm of ideas and the concrete reality of the sculpted form. It is through this intimate connection with the material that the sculptor is able to imbue the stone with life, transforming it from a cold, inert mass into a work of art that speaks to the human spirit.

4.2 A Crafted Language

The sculptor's vocabulary isn't one of words, but of actions. It's a language etched in steel and whispered in stone dust, a lexicon of pressure and release, of addition and subtraction. Understanding this language, this intimate dialogue between the sculptor and their material, is essential. It's about more than simply knowing the names of tools or the sequence of steps; it's about developing an intuitive feel for how the material responds to each touch, each strike, each considered pause. This chapter will delve into the specifics of that interaction, exploring the nuances of technique that transform raw material into evocative form.

Consider the point chisel, a tool of precision and force. Its sharp pyramid tip allows for controlled removal of material, enabling the sculptor to delineate sharp lines, carve intricate details, and create crisp, defined forms. The angle of attack, the force applied, and even the rhythm of the blows all contribute to the final result. A light touch might produce a delicate shaving, while a powerful strike could remove a substantial chunk, altering the form dramatically. Mastering this control, understanding the subtle interplay of force and finesse, is crucial for expressing one's artistic vision.

Then there's the tooth chisel, its broad, serrated edge ideal for removing larger amounts of material quickly and efficiently. It's the workhorse of the sculptor's toolkit, used for roughing out initial forms, establishing basic proportions, and preparing the surface for finer work. Its rhythmic bite leaves a textured surface, a testament to the energetic exchange between the sculptor and the stone. This texture can be further refined or left as a deliberate stylistic choice, adding another layer of visual interest to the piece.

The claw chisel, with its multiple points, offers yet another approach. It's particularly effective for creating textured surfaces, removing material in controlled bursts, leaving a characteristic stippled effect. This tool can be used to evoke a sense of movement, suggesting the flow of drapery or the ripple of muscles beneath the skin. Its versatility allows the sculptor to shift between broad strokes and delicate details, adapting to the specific demands of the form.

Beyond these fundamental tools, there's a whole universe of specialized chisels, each designed for a particular purpose. The flat chisel, for instance, is invaluable for smoothing surfaces and creating planar facets, while the rondel, with its rounded tip, allows for carving concave forms and fluid curves. Choosing the right tool for the task is part of the sculptor's skill, a nuanced understanding of how each instrument interacts with the stone.

However, tools alone do not a sculptor make. The true artistry lies in the hand that wields them, in the sensitivity and understanding that guides their application. It's the sculptor's intimate knowledge of the material, their ability to anticipate how the stone will fracture and yield, that truly shapes the work. This knowledge is acquired through patient practice, through countless hours of chipping and shaping, of observing and responding to the material's inherent qualities.

Furthermore, the sculptor's "crafted language" extends beyond the physical act of carving. It encompasses the entire process, from selecting the stone to conceiving the form, from the initial roughing out to the final polishing. It involves understanding the interplay of light and shadow, the balance of mass and void, the subtle nuances of texture and form. It's a holistic approach, a deep engagement with the material and the idea it embodies.

The act of sculpting is, in essence, a conversation. The sculptor poses a question with each strike of the chisel, and the stone responds in kind, revealing its inner nature, its inherent beauty. This dialogue continues until the form emerges, a tangible expression of the sculptor's vision, a testament to the power of this crafted language. It's a language that transcends words, speaking directly to the senses, inviting us to touch, to see, to feel the story etched in stone. This tactile and visual language allows the artist to communicate ideas, emotions, and stories that words sometimes fail to capture. The subtle curves, the rough textures, and the interplay of light and shadow all contribute to a narrative that unfolds in three dimensions, engaging the viewer in a powerful and immediate way. It's this ability to communicate beyond words, to connect with the viewer on a visceral level, that makes sculpture such a compelling and enduring art form. Through the mastery of this crafted language, the sculptor transforms inert matter into a vessel of meaning, a tangible expression of the human spirit.

4.3 Shaping the Void

Understanding negative space is paramount to successful sculpture. It's not simply about what you add, but what you take away. Think of the air around a figure, the gap between its legs, the hollow of a cupped hand. These aren't empty spaces; they are active participants in the overall composition, shaping the perceived form as much as the stone itself. Mastery lies in recognizing their potential and manipulating them with intention. Consider the classical Greek sculptures, where the drapery folds and the spaces between limbs create a rhythmic flow and enhance the sense of movement. This interplay of solid and void gives the work a lightness and dynamism that would be impossible to achieve with solid mass alone.

The concept of negative space extends beyond the immediately visible. It also encompasses the implied volume within a form. Imagine a closed fist. We understand the presence of the enclosed space, even though it's hidden from view. This implied volume contributes to the overall sense of weight and tension. Similarly, a partially opened door suggests a room beyond, inviting the viewer to imagine the unseen space and its potential contents. This ability to evoke a sense of something more, something beyond the tangible, is a powerful tool for the sculptor.

One effective method for training your eye to see negative space is to practice contour drawing. Focus on the outlines of an object, not its internal details. Trace the edges of the spaces around it, paying particular attention to how these shapes interact with and define the positive form. This exercise helps to shift your perspective, encouraging you to see the voids not as empty areas but as integral parts of the composition. Another helpful visualization technique is to imagine pouring water over your sculpture. Where would the water flow? Where would it pool? These imagined pathways can reveal the interplay of positive and negative space, helping you to refine the form and create a more dynamic and engaging piece.

As you work, consider the relationship between the negative spaces and the overall narrative of your piece. Do they create a sense of openness and invitation, or do they contribute to a feeling of enclosure and introspection? A figure huddled within a small, defined space might convey vulnerability or isolation, while a figure reaching outwards, interacting with the surrounding void, could suggest aspiration or connection with the wider world. The possibilities are endless.

Remember that the void isn't static. It changes with the viewer's perspective. As someone walks around a sculpture, the negative spaces shift and transform, revealing new relationships and creating a dynamic visual experience. This element of change over time adds another layer of complexity to the work, encouraging interaction and deeper engagement. Consider how the light plays across the surfaces and through the voids, casting shadows that further accentuate the interplay of positive and negative form.

Developing a sensitivity to negative space is an ongoing process. It requires careful observation, experimentation, and a willingness to embrace the unseen. By understanding the power of the void, you can elevate your sculpture beyond mere representation and create works that resonate with depth and meaning. Look at the work of Barbara Hepworth, whose pierced forms explore the dynamic relationship between solid and void with remarkable elegance. Study the sculptures of Henry Moore, whose reclining figures invite the viewer to explore the spaces within and around them. These artists masterfully employ negative space to create works that are both visually compelling and conceptually rich.

Observe the natural world. Notice the spaces between branches of a tree, the gaps in a rock formation, the negative shapes created by overlapping leaves. Nature is a master sculptor, and its creations offer endless inspiration for understanding the interplay of positive and negative space. By carefully observing these natural forms, you can develop a deeper appreciation for the role of the void in shaping our perception of the world.

Begin to incorporate these observations into your own work. Experiment with different approaches to shaping the void. Try carving deep recesses into your sculptures, creating areas of shadow and depth. Explore the use of open forms, allowing the surrounding space to penetrate and interact with the solid mass. Don't be afraid to take risks and push the boundaries of your understanding. The more you experiment, the more you will discover about the power of negative space to enhance your artistic expression.

5 Chapter 5: The Creative Process

The genesis of a sculpture isn't a singular event but a confluence of influences, a gradual accretion of experiences and observations that solidify into a tangible vision. It begins not with a chisel striking stone, but with a quiet stirring within, a nascent idea taking root in the fertile ground of the mind. This could be a fleeting image glimpsed in the dappled sunlight on a forest floor, the graceful arc of a bird in flight, or the weathered texture of an ancient wall. These sensory impressions, seemingly disparate, coalesce over time, weaving themselves into the fabric of the artist's consciousness. They become the raw materials of creation, awaiting the moment of ignition.

This "spark of inspiration," as it's often romanticized, is rarely a bolt from the blue. It's more often a gentle dawning, a gradual unveiling of an idea that has been slowly gestating. It's a process of attentive listening, of paying heed to the subtle whispers of the subconscious. It's about cultivating a receptive state of mind, allowing oneself to be permeated by the world's myriad forms and textures. This receptivity extends beyond the visual realm, encompassing all sensory experiences – the rustling of leaves, the coolness of water on skin, the weight of clay in one's hands. Each sensation contributes to the rich tapestry of inspiration, informing and enriching the creative process. From this wellspring of inspiration, the journey towards tangible form begins. The initial vision, often nebulous and undefined, requires careful nurturing and focused attention to take shape. This is where the sculptor's true work begins – the painstaking process of translating an internal vision into the external reality of stone. Sketchbooks become battlegrounds for competing ideas, filled with tentative lines and hastily scribbled notes. Clay maquettes, rough and malleable, allow for a three-dimensional exploration of form, a tactile dialogue with the emerging sculpture. This stage is characterized by constant refinement, a continuous cycle of experimentation and revision. It's a process of discovery, of uncovering the inherent potential within the material and allowing the form to reveal itself.

The transition from this malleable stage to the unyielding nature of stone demands a shift in approach. The sculptor must now engage with the specific qualities of the chosen material, its density, its grain, its inherent limitations and possibilities. This is not a battle of wills, but a collaborative endeavor, a respectful negotiation between artist and material. The sculptor learns to listen to the stone, to understand its unique character, and to work in harmony with its natural properties. This intimate understanding of the material informs every decision, every strike of the chisel, every nuanced curve and plane. The process becomes a dance, a carefully choreographed interplay between the sculptor's intention and the stone's resistance. The act of sculpting is not merely the removal of excess material, but the revelation of form that already exists within the stone. It's a process of subtraction that paradoxically leads to addition, a peeling away of layers to reveal the essence of the sculpture within. Each strike of the chisel is a deliberate act, a conscious decision that shapes not only the stone, but also the sculptor's understanding of the work. This dynamic interplay between intention and action is at the heart of the creative process, driving the evolution of the sculpture from raw material to finished form. It's a journey of constant learning and adaptation, a testament to the transformative power of human creativity in dialogue with the natural world. The final sculpture stands as a testament to this intricate process, a physical embodiment of the artist's vision, materialized through the patient and persistent dialogue with stone. It's a tangible record of the journey from inspiration's spark to realized form, a testament to the enduring power of human creativity to shape and be shaped by the world around us. The sculpture, in its final form, becomes a bridge between the internal world of the artist and the external world of the viewer, inviting contemplation and interpretation. It stands as a silent yet powerful expression of the human experience, a testament to our capacity to find meaning and beauty in the world, and to transform that vision into tangible form. The creative process, therefore, is not a linear progression, but a cyclical dance between inspiration, experimentation, and realization, a testament to the enduring human impulse to create and connect with the world through the transformative power of art.

5.1 Inspiration's Spark

The genesis of a sculpture isn't a singular event, but a confluence of influences, a gradual accumulation of experiences and observations that coalesce into a tangible vision. It's a process as much about recognizing the potential within the raw material as it is about the conscious act of creation. For me, inspiration often arises from an unexpected encounter – the way sunlight catches the edge of a cliff face, revealing the striations of geological time, or the smooth, worn surface of a river stone, whispering tales of constant flow. These moments, seemingly insignificant in their fleeting nature, lodge themselves in the subconscious, subtly shaping the creative landscape. They become seeds of ideas, waiting for the right conditions to germinate.

Inspiration also emerges from a deep engagement with the world around us. Active observation, a conscious effort to truly see the interplay of light and shadow, the delicate balance of forms in nature, and the subtle textures of everyday objects. A walk through a forest can become a study in contrasting textures – the rough bark of a tree against the delicate veins of a leaf. The curve of a bird's wing in flight might inspire the graceful sweep of a sculpted arm. This attentive observation isn't a passive act; it requires a conscious choice to engage with the world, to internalize its forms, and to translate those observations into a unique artistic language.

Furthermore, inspiration is nurtured by a constant exploration of artistic traditions and the work of other sculptors. Studying the masters, from Michelangelo to Barbara Hepworth, provides a crucial foundation, a framework for understanding the possibilities and limitations of the medium. Examining their approaches to form, composition, and the interplay of light and shadow can spark new ideas and challenge preconceived notions. It's not about imitation, but about absorbing the lessons of history, understanding the evolution of sculptural language, and using that knowledge to forge a distinct personal style. Each artist's voice adds to the ongoing conversation, contributing to the rich tapestry of sculptural expression.

The act of sketching, whether in a notebook or directly onto the stone itself, is an integral part of this inspirational process. It's a way of externalizing those internal images, of giving form to fleeting thoughts and nascent ideas. A quick charcoal sketch can capture the essence of a gesture, the dynamic tension of a pose, or the subtle curve of a line. These sketches aren't meant to be finished works; they are exploratory tools, a means of working through different possibilities, refining compositions, and experimenting with various approaches. They serve as a bridge between the ephemeral world of inspiration and the tangible reality of the stone.

Equally important is the willingness to embrace the unexpected, to allow for serendipity within the creative process. Sometimes, a flaw in the stone, a chance fracture, or an unforeseen challenge can lead to unexpected discoveries. These moments of unplanned divergence can push the work in new and exciting directions, forcing a reevaluation of the initial vision and opening up unforeseen possibilities. Embracing these unexpected turns requires flexibility and a willingness to let go of preconceived notions, allowing the material itself to guide the creative process.

Finally, inspiration requires a space for quiet contemplation, a time for the mind to wander and for ideas to incubate. This could be a solitary walk in nature, listening to music, or simply sitting in quiet reflection. It's in these moments of stillness, when the external world fades into the background, that the subconscious can come to the forefront, allowing for the synthesis of experiences and observations into a coherent artistic vision. It's a process of allowing the mind to make connections, to draw upon the vast reservoir of stored images, memories, and emotions, and to shape them into something new and meaningful. This period of incubation is essential for the germination of creative ideas, allowing them to take root and blossom into fully realized forms. It is the fertile ground from which inspiration springs, nurturing the spark that ignites the creative process. It's the silent dialogue between the artist and the muse, the quiet conversation that shapes the future of the stone.

5.2 From Vision to Form

The sculptor's journey begins not with chisel against stone, but with an image kindled within the mind's eye. This inner vision, often nebulous and fleeting, is the genesis of every sculpted form. It may be sparked by a fleeting glimpse of a natural scene – the majestic sweep of a mountain ridge, the delicate curve of a seashell, the weathered texture of ancient bark. Perhaps it arises from a poignant human interaction – the graceful gesture of a dancer, the serene expression of a loved one, the stoic strength of a weathered face. Or it could emerge from a purely abstract idea, a concept or emotion seeking tangible expression. Whatever its source, this initial spark is the raw material, the uncarved block from which the sculpture will eventually emerge. Capturing and nurturing this nascent vision is crucial to the entire creative process.

Holding onto that initial spark of inspiration requires a conscious effort. It is like cupping water in your hands – too tight a grip and it spills away, too loose and it slips through your fingers. Sketchbooks become indispensable companions, filled with quick studies and detailed drawings that attempt to fix the ephemeral vision onto paper. Clay, a more malleable medium, allows for a three-dimensional exploration of form, enabling the artist to translate the mental image into a tangible object. Small-scale maquettes, miniature versions of the intended sculpture, can be crafted in wax or plaster, providing a further opportunity to refine the composition and explore different perspectives. These preliminary stages are not merely preparatory steps, but integral parts of the creative process, allowing the artist to wrestle with the form, to understand its inherent dynamics, and to prepare for the demanding work ahead.

The transition from this fluid, exploratory phase to the immutable solidity of stone demands a shift in mindset. The sculptor must now consider the specific qualities of the chosen material – its density, its texture, its color, its veining. A piece of Carrara marble, with its luminous white purity, will lend itself to a different expression than a block of rough-hewn granite, imbued with a sense of ancient strength. The sculptor must learn to "see" the finished form within the raw material, to anticipate how the stone will respond to the chisel, how light will play across its surfaces. This intimate knowledge of the material is not acquired through textbooks or lectures, but through direct, physical engagement – the touch of the hand, the sound of the hammer, the dust rising from the carved surface.

The actual process of carving is a slow, deliberate dance between the sculptor and the stone. It is a conversation, a dialogue in which each action elicits a response. The sculptor removes material, revealing the form within, while the stone, in turn, reveals its own inherent character, its hidden flaws and unexpected beauties. This interplay requires patience, precision, and a deep understanding of the material's behavior. Each strike of the chisel must be purposeful, informed by both the initial vision and the evolving reality of the stone. There are moments of exhilarating discovery, when the form emerges as if by magic, and moments of frustrating setbacks, when the stone resists the sculptor's will, forcing a reassessment of the design.

This process of subtraction, of removing material to reveal form, can be seen as a metaphor for the creative process itself. We begin with a chaotic jumble of ideas, emotions, and influences. Through careful selection and refinement, we chip away at the excess, discarding the unnecessary, until the essential form is revealed. This act of refinement, of paring down to the core essence, is not a process of limitation, but one of liberation. By removing the superfluous, we allow the true form, the essential idea, to shine forth with greater clarity and power. It is a journey from the formless to the formed, from the vague to the precise, from the potential to the actual.

The final stages of carving involve a delicate balance between detail and overall form. The sculptor refines the surfaces, smooths the transitions, and adds the final touches that bring the piece to life. Light becomes a crucial element, shaping the contours, highlighting the textures, and creating an interplay of shadow and substance. The finished sculpture is not merely a representation of the initial vision, but a synthesis of that vision and the inherent qualities of the stone. It is a testament to the transformative power of the creative process, a tangible expression of the dialogue between the artist and the material. It stands as a silent witness to the journey from vision to form, a journey that embodies the essence of sculpting itself. It is a testament to the enduring power of human creativity to transform raw material into something meaningful and beautiful, a testament etched in stone for generations to come. The sculptor's hand, guided by vision and informed by the spirit of the material, has given birth to a new form, a new presence in the world.

6 Chapter 6: Art and Meaning

A sculpture, silent and still, speaks volumes. It whispers narratives through the language of form, engaging in a dialogue that transcends the spoken word. This silent narrative, woven into the very fabric of the stone, invites interpretation, offering a space for personal connection and shared understanding. Consider the curve of a limb, the tension in a torso, the subtle tilt of a head. Each element contributes to a story unfolding, a story told not through words, but through the evocative power of shape and form. The artist imbues the material with intention, but the viewer completes the narrative, bringing their own experiences and perspectives to bear on the work. This interplay between artist and audience, between creation and interpretation, lies at the heart of artistic meaning.

Interpretation, in the realm of sculpture, is a dynamic and multifaceted process. It's not about deciphering a singular, fixed meaning imposed by the artist, but rather about engaging in a personal exploration of the work. We bring our own cultural baggage, our emotional landscapes, and our individual histories to the encounter. A single sculpture can evoke a multitude of responses, sparking different associations and interpretations in each viewer. What one person perceives as strength, another might see as vulnerability. What resonates as peace for one, might evoke a sense of unease in another. This multiplicity of meaning enriches the artistic experience, transforming the sculpture into a mirror reflecting the diverse perspectives of its audience. The act of interpretation becomes a collaborative act, a conversation between the artwork and the individual.

Symbols, embedded within the sculpted form, add layers of complexity and depth to the narrative. A bird in flight might represent freedom or aspiration. A clenched fist could symbolize defiance or struggle. The flowing drapery of a garment can evoke grace or movement. These symbolic elements, often drawn from cultural and historical contexts, act as visual cues, guiding the viewer's interpretation and adding richness to the overall meaning of the work. However, the power of symbolism lies not in its fixed definitions, but in its capacity to evoke personal associations and resonate with individual experiences. A symbol, like the overall form of the sculpture, becomes a catalyst for personal reflection and meaning-making.

Art, in its purest form, is a dialogue. A sculpture, though static in its physical presence, engages in a dynamic exchange with the world around it. It converses with the space it inhabits, with the light that plays across its surfaces, and, most importantly, with the individuals who encounter it. This dialogue transcends time and culture, connecting us to the human experience across generations. A sculpture created centuries ago can still speak to us today, provoking emotions, challenging assumptions, and sparking new insights. It is in this ongoing conversation, this dynamic interplay between artwork and audience, that art finds its enduring power and relevance. The silent language of sculpture, though wordless, can communicate profound truths about the human condition.

Transcending the material is the ultimate aspiration of sculpture. While rooted in the physicality of stone, wood, or metal, a successful sculpture transcends its material limitations to evoke something more ethereal, something that touches the realm of the spiritual. It is through the skillful manipulation of form, the evocative use of symbolism, and the invitation to personal interpretation, that the sculptor achieves this transcendence. The stone ceases to be mere matter and becomes a vessel for meaning, a conduit for emotion, and a testament to the enduring power of human creativity. The cold, hard surface of the material is imbued with warmth and life, transformed into a tangible expression of the intangible. This ability to transcend the material, to touch the spirit through the manipulation of form, is the hallmark of truly great sculpture. It is in this transformative act that the essence of "Stone and Spirit" truly resides.

6.1 A Silent Narrative

Consider the silent conversation that unfolds between a sculpture and its observer. A sculpture, unlike a painting or a piece of music, occupies three dimensions. It demands physical space and invites interaction, a circumnavigation. The viewer is drawn not just to observe, but to explore – to trace the contours of the form, to consider the interplay of light and shadow, to feel the weight and texture of the material. This tangible presence gives sculpture a unique power to communicate, even without words, engaging the viewer in a silent dialogue. This dialogue is not a monologue delivered by the artist, but a collaborative interpretation, a meaning co-created by the observer and the work itself. The meaning isn't fixed; it shifts and evolves with each interaction, each new perspective.

This silent narrative, inherent in sculptural form, operates on multiple levels. The most immediate is the visual. The shape, the proportions, the interplay of positive and negative space – these elements create a visual language that speaks directly to our senses. A sweeping curve can evoke a sense of fluidity and grace, while a sharp angle might suggest tension or strength. The surface treatment, too, plays a crucial role. A highly polished surface reflects light, creating a sense of dynamism and ethereal beauty, while a rough, textured surface invites a more tactile experience, grounding the work in the physical realm. The chosen material also speaks volumes. The cool, smooth surface of marble conveys a different message than the rough, earthy texture of granite. Each material carries its own history, its own associations, adding layers of meaning to the finished work.

Beyond the purely visual, the narrative unfolds through the interplay of symbol and metaphor. A recurring motif, a particular gesture, the placement of a figure in space – these elements can be imbued with symbolic meaning, adding depth and complexity to the work. These symbols might draw upon cultural traditions, historical events, or personal experiences, creating a rich tapestry of meaning. A sculptor might use the image of a bird in flight to symbolize freedom or transcendence, or the intertwining of two forms to represent connection and interdependence. These symbolic layers enrich the narrative, inviting the viewer to delve deeper into the work's meaning. It's important to remember, though, that these symbols are not always fixed or universally understood. Their meaning can be fluid, open to interpretation, and dependent on the individual viewer's experiences and cultural background.

The setting of a sculpture also plays a vital role in shaping its silent narrative. A piece situated in a natural environment will interact with the surrounding landscape, the changing light, the elements. The same sculpture placed in a gallery setting will evoke a different response, its meaning shaped by the controlled environment and the proximity of other works. Even within a gallery, the specific placement, the lighting, the surrounding space – all these factors contribute to the viewer's experience and influence their interpretation of the work. A sculpture positioned in a dimly lit corner will evoke a different mood than one bathed in bright light. The space itself becomes part of the narrative, a silent partner in the conversation between the artwork and the observer.

The act of interpretation, then, is not passive reception but an active engagement. The viewer brings their own experiences, their own cultural lens, their own emotional state to the encounter. They project their own stories onto the silent form, creating a unique and personal interpretation. This dynamic interplay between the artwork and the observer is what gives sculpture its enduring power. It's a conversation that continues long after the artist has finished their work, a silent narrative that unfolds with each new encounter. The sculpture becomes a vessel for meaning, a catalyst for reflection, inviting us to engage not just with the physical form, but with the deeper questions it evokes about ourselves and our place in the world. This active participation is crucial to the experience of sculpture. It is in this space, in this shared creation of meaning, that the true power of the silent narrative resides.

The silence of sculpture is not an absence of meaning, but a profound invitation. It's an invitation to look closely, to listen with our eyes, to engage with the material world in a tangible and meaningful way. It's an invitation to participate in a dialogue that transcends words, a silent narrative that speaks volumes. It is in this silence that the deepest connections are forged, the most profound meanings revealed. The quiet power of sculpture lies in its ability to spark this silent conversation, to invite us into a world of meaning that exists beyond the realm of language. This quiet strength, this ability to communicate without words, is what makes sculpture a unique and enduring art form. It is a testament to the power of form, the eloquence of silence, and the enduring human need to connect with something beyond ourselves. In the stillness of stone, we find a voice that speaks to the deepest parts of our being.

6.2 Interpreting Form

Understanding a sculpture isn't about deciphering a hidden code. It's about engaging in a sensory conversation with the form itself. Consider the interplay of light and shadow across the surface. How does the light define the curves and planes, revealing the artist's deliberate manipulations of the material? Observe the textures: rough, smooth, polished. Do these textures evoke a particular feeling or memory? A rough, unfinished surface might suggest rawness or vulnerability, while a highly polished surface could convey elegance or strength. These tactile qualities are not accidental. They contribute to the overall narrative the sculpture presents.

Walk around the piece. Don't just stand in one spot. Movement allows you to experience the sculpture from multiple perspectives, revealing how its form changes in relation to your position. Notice how certain angles emphasize specific details while others obscure them. This dynamic interplay between viewer and object is crucial to interpreting the work's meaning. Is there a particular vantage point that feels more significant than others? Why? Perhaps the artist intentionally designed the sculpture to be viewed from a specific angle, guiding the viewer's gaze and shaping their understanding.

Consider the sculpture's scale in relation to your own body. A monumental work might inspire awe or a sense of being dwarfed, while a smaller, more intimate piece might encourage closer inspection and a feeling of connection. This relationship between scale and the viewer's physical presence influences the emotional impact of the artwork. Does the sculpture tower over you, demanding attention? Or does it invite a more intimate encounter, encouraging you to lean in and explore its nuances? The artist's choice of scale is a deliberate decision that shapes the viewer's experience.

Think about the negative space – the empty areas surrounding and within the sculpture. Negative space isn't simply emptiness. It's an active component of the composition, shaping the positive forms and contributing to the overall visual impact. Observe how the negative space interacts with the solid mass, creating a sense of balance or tension. Does it frame the subject, drawing attention to specific features? Or does it create a sense of movement or flow, guiding the viewer's eye through the composition?

Reflect on the material itself. What kind of stone is it? Is it marble, granite, limestone? Each stone has unique properties – color, texture, density – that influence its aesthetic qualities and symbolic meaning. Marble, for example, has long been associated with purity and timelessness, while granite suggests strength and permanence. These inherent qualities of the material contribute to the overall message conveyed by the sculpture. Does the stone's natural veining or coloration play a role in the composition? Does the material's inherent strength or fragility inform the piece's emotional impact?

Context is crucial. Research the artist's background and the historical period in which the sculpture was created. Understanding the artist's intentions and the cultural context can provide valuable insights into the work's meaning. Were there specific historical events or artistic movements that influenced the artist? What were the prevailing social and cultural norms of the time? Consider how these factors might have shaped the artist's vision and the sculpture's form. Don't be afraid to bring your own experiences and interpretations to the work. Art is a subjective experience, and there is no single "correct" way to understand a sculpture. Your personal background, emotions, and perspectives will shape your interpretation, and that's perfectly valid. What feelings does the sculpture evoke in you? What memories or associations does it bring to mind? Allow yourself to connect with the work on a personal level, and trust your own intuitive responses.

Interpreting a sculpture is an ongoing dialogue, a process of discovery that unfolds over time. The more you look, the more you see. The more you reflect, the deeper your understanding becomes. It's a journey of exploration, an opportunity to connect with the artist's vision and engage with the profound expressive power of form. Embrace the ambiguity, the open-endedness of the experience. Let your curiosity guide you, and allow yourself to be moved by the stone's silent story.

6.3 The Power of Symbol

A sculptor imbues a work with symbolic language, layering meaning into the seemingly inert material. We choose stone not just for its physical properties, but for its cultural and historical resonance. Granite, with its unyielding strength, might symbolize permanence or resilience. Alabaster, with its translucent fragility, might represent ephemerality or vulnerability. Even the color of the stone carries weight – the deep black of basalt evoking mystery and the warm tones of sandstone suggesting earth and stability. This mindful selection of material is the first step in constructing a symbolic vocabulary.

Consider the human form in sculpture. Throughout history, artists have explored the human figure as a vessel for symbolic expression. The idealized proportions of classical Greek sculpture conveyed notions of beauty, harmony, and divine order. The contorted figures of Renaissance Pietàs embody grief, suffering, and spiritual transcendence. The expressive postures of modern figurative works can reflect psychological states, social commentary, or personal narratives. Even the absence of the figure, a negative space carved into the stone, can be powerfully symbolic, hinting at loss, absence, or the unseen forces shaping our lives.

Beyond the human form, the natural world offers a rich source of symbolic inspiration. Animals, plants, and celestial bodies have held symbolic significance across cultures for millennia. The soaring flight of a bird might represent freedom or spiritual aspiration. The unfurling of a flower could symbolize growth, beauty, or the fleeting nature of life. The cyclical phases of the moon might evoke themes of change, renewal, or the feminine principle. By incorporating these natural motifs, a sculptor can tap into a universal language of symbolism, creating works that resonate deeply with viewers.

Abstract forms, too, hold symbolic potential. The interplay of lines, planes, and volumes can evoke a range of emotions and ideas. A spiraling form might suggest growth, expansion, or the journey of life. A sharp, angular form could convey tension, conflict, or a sense of dynamism. A smooth, rounded form might represent wholeness, harmony, or the embrace of the feminine. Through careful manipulation of form, a sculptor can communicate complex ideas without resorting to literal representation.

The placement and context of a sculpture also contribute to its symbolic meaning. A monumental sculpture in a public square might represent civic pride, historical commemoration, or shared values. A small, intimate sculpture in a private home might evoke personal memories, spiritual contemplation, or a sense of sanctuary. Even the interaction of light and shadow on a sculpture can enhance its symbolic impact, creating an ever-shifting interplay of meaning. Think of a sunlit figure appearing to emerge from the darkness, symbolizing hope or enlightenment.

Ultimately, the power of symbol in sculpture lies in its capacity to transcend the purely material. Stone becomes a vehicle for expressing intangible concepts, connecting us to deeper layers of meaning and understanding. A successful sculpture speaks not only to the intellect but also to the emotions and the spirit. It invites viewers to engage in a dialogue with the work, to interpret its symbols, and to discover their own personal connections to the art. This interactive process is what makes sculpture such a potent and enduring form of human expression. The act of interpreting a symbol is a creative act in itself, completing the circle of artistic communication between sculptor and viewer. This shared experience, this exchange of meaning across time and space, is at the heart of the power of symbol. It's a testament to the enduring human need to find meaning in the world around us, to connect with something larger than ourselves, and to express the complexities of the human condition through the beauty and permanence of stone.

6.4 Art as Dialogue

Sculpture, in its most profound expression, transcends mere representation and enters into a dialogue. It converses not only with the viewer but also with the material itself, the surrounding space, and the echoes of history embedded within the stone. This dialogue is a multifaceted exchange, a continuous interplay of intention, perception, and interpretation. The sculptor initiates the conversation, imbuing the raw material with a nascent form, a whisper of an idea. Yet, the stone itself responds, its inherent qualities—its density, texture, and color—influencing the direction of the work.

Consider the subtle veins running through a block of marble, each a unique record of geological time. These markings are not imperfections but rather opportunities for dialogue, invitations to incorporate the stone's history into the emerging narrative. A skilled sculptor learns to listen to these whispers, allowing them to inform the evolving form. Perhaps a vein suggests a curve in a limb, the flow of drapery, or the ripple of water. This responsiveness to the material creates a sense of organic unity, a harmonious blending of human intention and natural form. It's a dance between artist and material, a push and pull that ultimately shapes the final expression.

The dialogue extends beyond the intimate exchange between sculptor and stone to encompass the viewer. A finished sculpture stands as an open invitation to interpretation, a question posed in three dimensions. Each observer brings their unique experiences, perspectives, and cultural baggage to the encounter, shaping their understanding of the work. What one person sees as strength, another may perceive as vulnerability. A curve might evoke fluidity and grace, or perhaps tension and restraint. This multiplicity of interpretations is not a weakness but a strength, enriching the artwork's meaning and ensuring its continued relevance across time and cultures.

This interplay of perspectives creates a dynamic, ever-evolving conversation around the artwork. The sculpture becomes a focal point for shared experience, prompting discussion, debate, and even disagreement. It acts as a catalyst for connection, fostering a sense of community around a shared object of contemplation. This communal aspect of art is crucial, transforming a solitary act of creation into a shared cultural experience. It moves beyond the realm of individual interpretation and enters the public sphere, becoming a part of the collective consciousness.

Furthermore, the dialogue extends beyond the present moment, reaching into the past and projecting into the future. A sculpture, particularly one crafted from enduring materials like stone, carries within it the echoes of its creation. The sculptor's hand, the tools used, the environment in which it was made—all leave their subtle imprint on the finished work. These traces become part of the sculpture's story, adding layers of meaning that resonate across generations. A weathered surface might speak of the passage of time, while a carefully polished plane might reflect the artist's meticulous attention to detail.

Looking ahead, the sculpture also enters into a dialogue with the future. Its physical presence endures, becoming a silent witness to the unfolding of history. Future generations will encounter the work, bringing their own perspectives and interpretations to bear. The sculpture's meaning will continue to evolve, shaped by the changing cultural landscape and the individual experiences of those who encounter it. This ongoing dialogue ensures the artwork's enduring relevance, its ability to speak to new audiences across the span of time.

Finally, the concept of dialogue in sculpture highlights the interconnectedness of all things. The stone itself is a product of geological forces, shaped by the earth's slow, relentless processes. The sculptor, in turn, is shaped by their environment, culture, and personal experiences. The viewer brings their own unique history to the encounter, and the sculpture itself becomes a part of the ongoing cultural narrative. This intricate web of influences creates a rich tapestry of meaning, demonstrating that art is not created in isolation but arises from a complex interplay of forces. It is this interconnectedness that gives sculpture its power to move us, to challenge us, and to connect us to something larger than ourselves. The quiet conversation between stone and spirit continues, resonating through time and space.

6.5 Transcending Material

The sculptor, through intimate interaction with the stone, engages in an act of elevation. We strive not merely to replicate form, but to imbue it with something beyond, something intangible yet profoundly felt. This transcendence is not achieved through grand gestures or elaborate techniques, but through a subtle shift in perspective, a recognition of the inherent energy residing within the material itself. We find ourselves conduits, channeling a force that flows through us, transforming the inert into the evocative. Consider the human form, a recurring motif in sculpture throughout history. We don't simply carve muscles and bone; we attempt to capture the essence of humanity—the spirit, the emotion, the ephemeral qualities that define our existence. This requires a deep understanding, not just of anatomy, but of the human condition itself.

The act of sculpting, then, becomes a meditation, a communion with the material and the subject it represents. Each strike of the chisel, each caress of the rasp, is imbued with intention, with a desire to unveil the hidden potential within the stone. We are not imposing our will upon the material, but rather collaborating with it, allowing its inherent properties to guide our hand. This collaborative process extends beyond the physical interaction with the stone. It encompasses the surrounding environment, the history embedded within the material, and the cultural context in which the work is created. A sculpture of a figure, for instance, might draw upon classical ideals of beauty, while simultaneously reflecting the anxieties and aspirations of our contemporary world.

This interplay between tradition and innovation, between the tangible and the intangible, is what elevates sculpture beyond mere representation. It allows us to engage with complex ideas, to explore profound emotions, and to connect with something larger than ourselves. The finished piece stands as a testament to this transformative process, a physical manifestation of the sculptor's inner vision. It speaks a silent language, inviting the viewer to participate in the ongoing dialogue between artist, material, and meaning. The viewer, in turn, brings their own experiences and interpretations to the work, further enriching its significance. This shared experience, this unspoken communication, is at the heart of art's power to transcend the purely material.

The process of transcending the material is deeply intertwined with the concept of memory. Stone, in its permanence, becomes a repository of time, holding within its structure the echoes of past events and experiences. A weathered surface might evoke the passage of centuries, while a polished plane can suggest the immediacy of the present moment. This interplay between past and present allows us to explore the ephemeral nature of human existence, to grapple with the complexities of time and memory. Through the careful manipulation of form and texture, we can imbue the stone with a sense of narrative, a story that unfolds silently within the viewer's mind. This narrative may be personal, drawing upon the sculptor's own memories and experiences, or it may be universal, exploring themes that resonate across cultures and generations.

The pursuit of transcendence in sculpture is a lifelong journey, a continuous exploration of the boundaries between material and spirit. It demands not only technical skill and artistic vision, but also a deep understanding of the human condition. It is a process of discovery, of unveiling the hidden potential within ourselves and the world around us. Ultimately, the goal is not to create something beautiful, but to create something meaningful, something that speaks to the very core of our being. This meaning might not always be readily apparent, it might reside in the subtle nuances of form, in the interplay of light and shadow, or in the evocative power of the material itself. But it is this inherent meaning, this underlying spirit, that elevates the sculpture beyond the realm of the purely material and transforms it into a work of art. The enduring power of sculpture lies in its ability to evoke a sense of wonder, to provoke thought, and to connect us with something greater than ourselves.

7 Chapter 7: Reflections on Legacy

The sculptor's hand, though long stilled, speaks through the enduring presence of stone. A life's work, etched into the unyielding material, becomes a dialogue across generations. This conversation transcends the immediate, reaching into a future the artist may never witness. We, the inheritors of these sculpted narratives, participate in a continuing exchange, adding our own interpretations to the stories embedded within the stone. It's a testament to the power of art to bridge temporal divides, connecting us to the past and projecting forward into the unknown.

Consider the weathered surface of a centuries-old statue, its contours softened by time and touch. Each imperfection, each subtle erosion, tells a tale. The play of light across its surface reveals not just the artist's intent but also the slow, relentless hand of time. This accumulation of years adds another layer of meaning, enriching the original narrative with the whispers of history. The statue becomes a palimpsest, carrying within it the echoes of countless interactions, a silent chronicle of human experience. It speaks to the enduring power of human creation, a stubborn resistance to oblivion.

This notion of legacy is not solely confined to monumental works or public art. A small, intricately carved amulet, passed down through generations, holds a similar power, albeit on a more intimate scale. It becomes a tangible link to ancestry, a physical embodiment of familial memory. The warmth of the stone against skin connects the present wearer to a lineage of touch, a shared experience stretching across decades or even centuries. These objects become more than mere adornments; they are vessels of memory, imbued with the stories of those who held them before.

The passage of time affects not only the stone itself but also our perception of it. A contemporary sculpture, sleek and modern, may speak to our present moment, reflecting current anxieties and aspirations. Yet, as time marches on, its meaning will inevitably shift. Future generations will view it through the lens of their own experiences, applying their own cultural context to its interpretation. What we see as avant-garde may become classic, and what we consider timeless may eventually seem dated. This evolution of meaning is inherent in the nature of art, a dynamic interaction between creator, object, and observer across the span of time.

Stone, in its very essence, is a recorder of time. Geological processes, spanning millennia, shape its form and texture. The sculptor, in turn, intervenes in this ancient narrative, imposing human will upon the material. This interplay between geological time and human intervention imbues the work with a unique depth, a resonance that transcends the purely aesthetic. It's a recognition that the stone itself possesses a history, a story that predates the artist's vision and extends beyond their lifespan.

Therefore, the sculptor's legacy is not merely about the creation of enduring objects. It is about engaging in a dialogue with time itself. It's about contributing to the ongoing conversation about human experience, expressed through the medium of stone. This dialogue continues long after the sculptor's hand has fallen silent, echoing through the ages in the enduring presence of their creations. It is a testament to the human desire to leave a mark, to connect with something larger than oneself, and to communicate across the vast expanse of time.

The act of sculpting, then, becomes an act of both creation and preservation. The artist, in shaping the stone, also shapes their own legacy. They imbue the material with a portion of their own spirit, their own understanding of the world. This essence remains, embedded within the stone, a silent story waiting to be discovered and reinterpreted by future generations. The true measure of an artist's legacy, therefore, lies not only in the physical endurance of their work but also in the enduring resonance of its meaning.

This resonance is amplified by the very nature of stone. Unlike more ephemeral materials, stone possesses an inherent sense of permanence. It stands as a defiant counterpoint to the fleeting nature of human existence, offering a tangible connection to the past and a hopeful projection into the future. This inherent durability lends a certain gravitas to stone sculpture, making it a powerful medium for exploring themes of legacy and enduring presence.

Moreover, the placement of a sculpture, particularly in public spaces, further contributes to its legacy. A work situated within a specific environment becomes intertwined with the history and identity of that place. It witnesses the unfolding of events, the ebb and flow of human activity, becoming a silent observer of the changing landscape. This integration into the fabric of a community imbues the sculpture with a shared meaning, transforming it from a mere object into a collective touchstone.

Finally, the sculptor's legacy extends beyond the individual works they create. It encompasses the inspiration they ignite in others, the conversations they spark, and the impact they have on the evolution of their art form. Their contributions ripple outwards, influencing subsequent generations of artists and shaping the very language of sculpture. This intangible legacy, though difficult to quantify, is perhaps the most profound and enduring of all. It is the enduring echo of a life devoted to the pursuit of beauty, meaning, and connection through the timeless medium of stone.

7.1 Enduring Presence

Consider the pyramids of Giza. Millennia have passed, dynasties have risen and fallen, yet these colossal structures remain, testaments to human ambition and ingenuity. Their enduring presence speaks not only of the pharaohs they entombed but also of the countless hands that labored to raise them, stone by painstaking stone. This very permanence, this ability to withstand the ravages of time, imbues stone sculpture with a unique power. It offers a form of artistic immortality, a chance to communicate across generations, to leave a tangible mark on the world.

This enduring presence extends beyond grand monuments. Consider the worn steps of an ancient temple, smoothed by the passage of countless feet. Each individual who traversed those stones contributed, however minutely, to their present form. The stones hold the echoes of their footsteps, a silent record of lives lived. Similarly, a small, intricately carved figure, tucked away in a museum, can possess a remarkable presence. It holds the energy of its creator, their intentions and aspirations, preserved within the material itself. It whispers stories of a specific time and place, inviting us to connect with the past.

The concept of enduring presence is inextricably linked to the materials we choose. Granite, basalt, marble—each possesses its own distinct character, its own inherent lifespan. Some stones weather and erode, acquiring a patina that speaks to the passage of time. Others remain remarkably pristine, their surfaces seemingly untouched by the elements. The sculptor, in choosing their material, makes a conscious decision about the intended lifespan of their work. Are they striving for timeless perfection, or embracing the inevitable changes wrought by time? This choice becomes an integral part of the artwork's narrative.

But enduring presence is not solely about physical permanence. It also encompasses the impact a work of art has on the viewer, the emotional resonance it creates. A sculpture can become a focal point for community gatherings, a place of solace and reflection, a symbol of shared values. It can inspire awe, provoke thought, or evoke powerful memories. In this way, a sculpture's presence transcends its physical form and becomes embedded within the cultural landscape. It's a dialogue between the artist, the material, and the observer, a conversation that continues long after the artist's hand has stilled.

Think of the public sculptures that inhabit our cities. They become landmarks, meeting places, points of reference. They interact with the changing light and the surrounding environment, their presence shifting throughout the day and across the seasons. They become woven into the fabric of daily life, their familiarity breeding a sense of comfort and connection. This ongoing interaction with the community is a vital aspect of their enduring presence.

The pursuit of enduring presence also involves a conscious effort to create work that resonates with future generations. This doesn't necessarily mean adhering to traditional aesthetics or striving for universal appeal. Rather, it requires an honesty of expression, a commitment to conveying something meaningful through the chosen medium. It's about creating work that speaks to the human condition, to our shared experiences of joy, sorrow, hope, and despair. It's about grappling with the big questions—questions of identity,

purpose, and our place in the universe.
Consider prehistoric cave paintings. Created in the flickering light of torches, these images of animals and human figures offer a glimpse into the minds of our ancestors. They communicate across vast stretches of time, revealing fundamental aspects of human nature. Though the artists remain anonymous, their work endures, a testament to the enduring power of artistic expression.
Ultimately, the enduring presence of a sculpture lies in its ability to connect with the human spirit. It's about creating something that transcends the purely decorative and speaks to something deeper within us. It's about crafting a work that invites contemplation, sparks dialogue, and leaves a lasting impression on the viewer's soul. It's about forging a connection between the ephemeral and the eternal, between the fleeting moment of creation and the enduring power of stone. It's about creating a legacy that will continue to resonate long after we are gone. This, perhaps, is the ultimate aspiration of the sculptor—to leave a mark on the world, a testament to the enduring power of human creativity.

7.2 The Passage of Time

The sculptor, unlike many other artists, works with a medium that explicitly acknowledges time. We don't create ephemeral images on canvas or fleeting melodies in air. We carve into a substance that has already witnessed millennia, a material that will likely outlast our own fleeting existence. This awareness of time permeates the entire creative process, from the initial selection of the stone to the final placement of the finished piece. It shapes our understanding of the work's meaning and its potential for dialogue across generations. We are, in a sense, collaborators with time itself, engaging in a conversation that spans centuries.

Consider the geological timescales embedded within a block of marble. Its very structure bears witness to epochs of pressure and transformation, to the slow, relentless movement of continents and the ebb and flow of ancient oceans. When we begin to carve, we are not simply shaping a form, but interacting with this vast history. We are adding our own brief mark to a narrative that began long before us and will continue long after we are gone. This perspective instills a sense of humility, a recognition that our work is but a small contribution to the ongoing story of the stone.

The act of sculpting is, in itself, a dialogue with time. The slow, deliberate process of removing material, of revealing the form within, requires patience and a willingness to surrender to the stone's own rhythm. There is no rushing the process; each strike of the chisel, each pass of the rasp, is a negotiation with the material and with the passage of time itself. This gradual unfolding of the form mirrors the slow, steady processes of nature, the weathering of rock, the growth of mountains. We learn to appreciate the value of slowness, the power of incremental change. We begin to understand that true creation cannot be hurried.

This awareness of time extends beyond the act of creation. It informs our understanding of the sculpture's potential for endurance. We choose stone, in part, for its durability, for its ability to withstand the ravages of time. We envision our work persisting through generations, becoming a part of the landscape, a silent witness to the unfolding of human history. This is not a desire for personal immortality, but rather a recognition of the power of art to connect us to something larger than ourselves, to transcend the limitations of our individual lifespans.

The weathered surfaces of ancient sculptures, the patina acquired through centuries of exposure to the elements, these are not signs of decay, but rather testaments to the passage of time. They tell stories of changing climates, of shifting cultures, of the enduring presence of human creativity. These marks of time add depth and richness to the work, connecting it to the broader sweep of history. They remind us that even as time passes, even as civilizations rise and fall, the human impulse to create endures.

The placement of a sculpture, too, is informed by this awareness of time. We consider how the work will interact with its environment over time, how it will be shaped by the elements, how it will become integrated into the landscape. We might choose a location where the sculpture will be exposed to the wind and rain, allowing nature to slowly etch its own marks upon the surface. Or we might situate the piece within a sheltered space, protecting it from the elements in the hope that it will remain unchanged for centuries to come. In either case, we are acknowledging the inevitable passage of time and its impact on the work.

Ultimately, the sculptor's engagement with time is not about resisting its passage, but about embracing its transformative power. We accept that our work, like everything else in the world, is subject to the forces of change and decay. But we also recognize that this impermanence is what gives life meaning. It is the fleeting nature of our existence that makes each moment precious, each creative act a testament to the enduring human spirit. By working with a material that embodies the passage of time, we are reminded of the profound connection between creation and destruction, between memory and forgetting, between the ephemeral and the eternal. We learn to appreciate the beauty of impermanence, the power of stone to bear witness to the ongoing story of time itself.

7.3 Stone's Silent Story

Stone holds a unique position in the dialogue of time. Unlike flesh and bone, it resists the swift erosion of years, standing as a stark counterpoint to our own fleeting existence. This inherent permanence imbues stone with a certain gravity, a silent power that speaks volumes across generations. It becomes a repository of memory, not just for the artist who shaped it, but for the cultures and civilizations that have risen and fallen around it. Consider the weathered surfaces of ancient megaliths, the intricate carvings adorning forgotten temples – each groove, each fracture, whispers tales of lives lived, beliefs held, and empires crumbled. This is the silent story of stone, a narrative etched not in ink or spoken word, but in the very fabric of the material itself.

This narrative is further enriched by the deliberate interventions of the artist. We impose our own fleeting moments onto the stone's enduring presence, seeking to create a bridge between the ephemeral and the eternal. Each chisel mark, each polished surface, represents a conscious act, a fleeting thought made tangible. We imbue the stone with our own stories, our hopes, our fears, creating a palimpsest of meaning layered upon the existing tapestry of time. The sculpture becomes a convergence point, a meeting place between the artist's transient life and the stone's enduring stillness. It's a conversation whispered across millennia, a dialogue between the present and the deep past.

Think of the worn steps of a public fountain, smoothed by countless hands over centuries. These stones bear witness to generations of shared experiences: joyous celebrations, quiet moments of reflection, hurried footsteps on daily errands. They absorb the energy of the community, becoming imbued with the collective memory of a place. Similarly, a tombstone, weathered and moss-covered, holds within it the essence of a single life, a silent testament to a unique individual who once walked among us. It's a tangible link to the past, a physical embodiment of remembrance.

The sculptor's act of shaping stone is, therefore, a deeply symbolic one. It's an attempt to capture something intangible, to freeze a moment in time and preserve it for posterity. We strive to translate fleeting emotions, abstract ideas, and personal experiences into the enduring language of stone. This translation is never perfect, of course, but it's in the striving, in the wrestling with the material, that the true meaning emerges. The imperfections, the subtle variations in texture and color, these are the marks of the artist's hand, the evidence of their struggle to communicate across time. They add depth and complexity to the stone's silent story, enriching the narrative with the human element.

This enduring presence of stone offers a unique perspective on our own mortality. Faced with the stone's immutability, we are forced to confront the fleeting nature of our own existence. This can be a humbling experience, a reminder of the larger forces at play in the universe. But it can also be a source of inspiration. By engaging with a material that transcends our own lifespan, we tap into a deeper well of creativity, a sense of connection to something larger than ourselves. We become part of a continuum, a chain of artists and creators stretching back through time.

The legacy we leave behind in stone is not just about the physical object itself, but about the stories it tells, the emotions it evokes, and the connections it forges. It's about the dialogue we initiate with future generations, a dialogue that continues long after we are gone. The stone remains, a silent witness to our passage, a testament to the enduring power of human creativity. It's a reminder that even in the face of time's relentless march, something of ourselves can endure. This, perhaps, is the greatest lesson that stone's silent story can teach us. It whispers of permanence in a world of change, of connection in a world of isolation, of meaning in a world often perceived as meaningless. It is a story worth listening to, a story that continues to unfold with each passing year, each weathered surface, each touch of a human hand.

www.ingramcontent.com/pod-product-compliance
Ingram Content Group UK Ltd.
Pitfield, Milton Keynes, MK11 3LW, UK
UKHW021436240125
4283UKWH00041B/635